by

Doug DuBosque

For my wife,
friend,
patient editor,
and child of the desert,
Susan Joyce DuBosque

-D.D.

Published by Peel Productions.

Printed in Singapore

3 5 7 9 8 6 4

Library of Congress Cataloging-in-Publication Data

DuBosque, D. C.
Draw desert animals / by Doug DuBosque
p. cm.
Includes index.
Summary: Offers step-by-step instructions for drawing various desert animals.
ISBN 0-939217-26-0
1. Desert Animals in art--Juvenile literature. 2. Drawing--Technique--Juvenile literature. [1. Desert Animals in art. 2. Drawing--technique.] I. Title.
NC783.8.D47D83
743'.6--dc20 95-51693

Distributed to the trade and art markets in North America by

North Light Books,
an imprint of F&W Publications, Inc.
4700 East Galbraith Road
Cincinnati, OH 45236

(800) 289-0963

DRAW
DESERT Animals

A few thoughts before you start...

Deserts – cool!

The deserts, or dry places, of the world hold plenty of surprises for those who explore them. Let's do that with a pencil!

Draw Desert Animals shows you how to draw fascinating creatures, step by step. You may find some of the drawings quite easy. Others will be challenges.

What do you need?

- PENCIL
  (2B or 3B will work well)
- PENCIL SHARPENER
- ERASER
  (kneadable works best)
- PAPER
  (test of quality: how easily can you erase on it?)
- PLACE TO DRAW
  Good light, no distractions.

What do you really need?

- POSITIVE ATTITUDE
  Forget *"I can't."*
  Say, "I'm learning." "I'm figuring this out." "I did this part well; now I'm going to work on the harder part...."

"...and I'm not stopping *until I get it RIGHT!"*

1

2

3

Think of drawing in three stages.

First

LOOK carefully at the desert animal you wish to draw! See the shapes and pieces and how they fit together.

Then, **lightly sketch** the shapes in the right place.

When you sketch lightly, you can easily correct any mistakes before they ruin your drawing.

Second

Make sure you have all the shapes and pieces in the right place:

- **adjust** lines
- **redraw** pieces that don't look right
- **erase** sketch lines you no longer need.

Third

Spend as much time as you need to make your drawing jump off the page:

- **darken** lines at emphasis points: joints, feet, points of claws, horns, spikes, eyes...
- add **fur**, **feathers**, or **scales...**
- add **shading**...
- **clean up** any smudges with your eraser...
- **Date and save** your drawing in a portfolio (see p.62).

Just so you know...

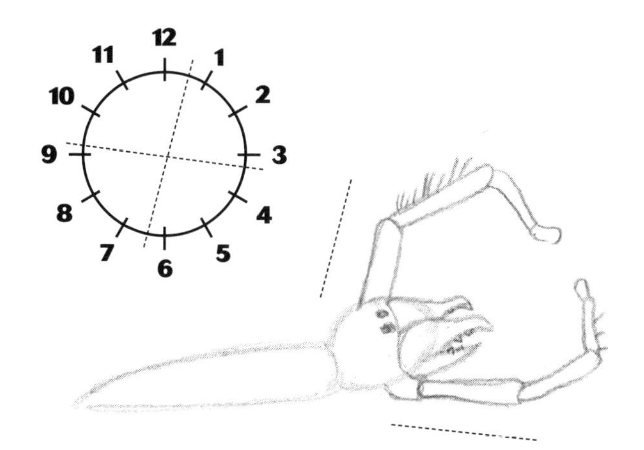

CLOCK FACES appear from time to time. Use them as a reference to see the tilt of ovals, legs, and other angles in the drawing.

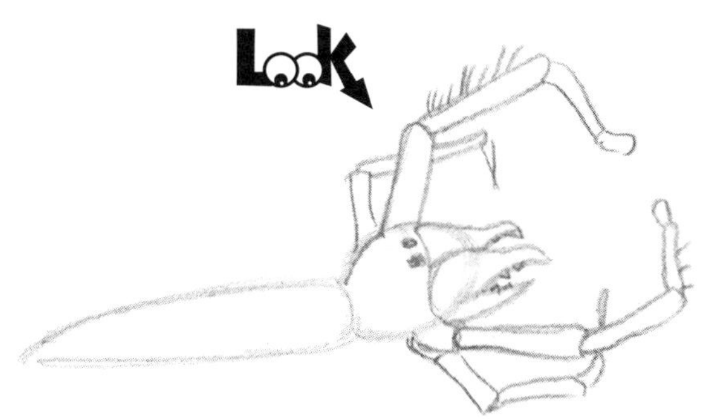

LOOK signs point out visual elements of the drawing–in this example, where one part overlaps another.

LABELS will help you identify the parts of the animal mentioned in the text.

And now, let's

Addax antelope

ALWAYS SKETCH LIGHTLY AT FIRST!

Addax nasomaculatus

Africa. Height: .9 – 1.2 m (3 – 4 ft)

An addax never drinks, getting all the moisture it needs from its food. Its large, wide-spreading hooves are adapted to walking on soft sand. Addax are nomads, traveling in herds of 20 to 200. They seem to have a special ability to locate the patches of desert vegetation that suddenly sprout after a downpour. Color varies from animal to animal, but they all have a patch of dark brown hair on the forehead.

1) Begin the addax by lightly sketching two ovals. Compare the tilt of the back leg oval to the clock face. Draw lines to connect the ovals, top and bottom.

2) Sketch a circle for the head, centered at the top of the shoulder. Sketch a smaller circle for the nose and mouth. Add ears.

   Draw jagged lines to connect the head to the body.

3) Draw the eyes–**look** at the way one sits on the edge of the circle, and one doesn't. Add curved guide lines for the facial pattern.

   Sketch small, light circles for the leg joints. Draw the front and rear legs. Notice how the tilt of the oval shows you the angle of the top of the rear leg.

   Add the tail.

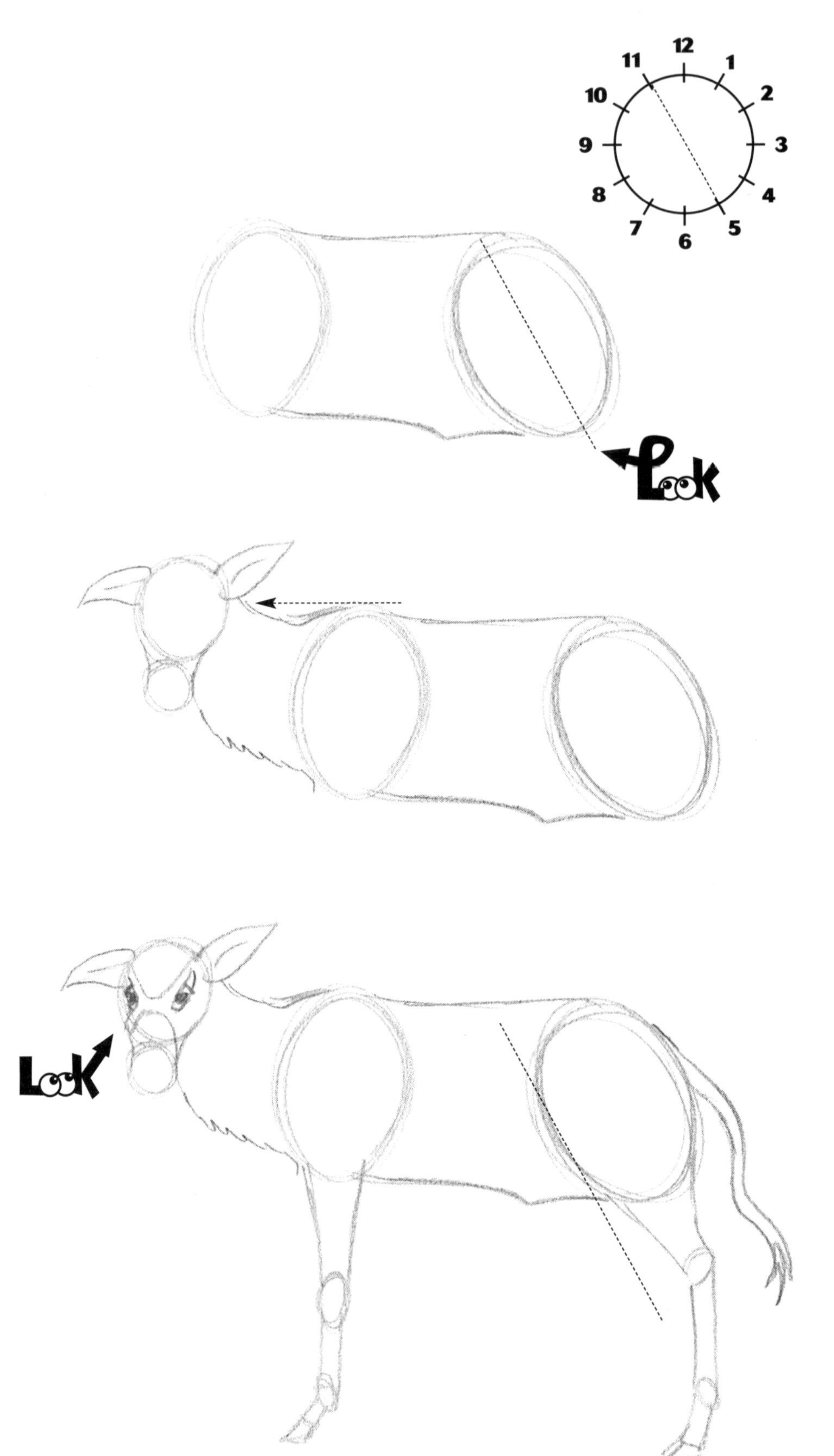

4) Lightly draw the graceful, spiralling horns. Once you have them right, begin to add small curved lines for the ridges on them. Add nostrils and the mouth. Shade the darker area of the face and ear.

Lightly sketch the joints and limbs of the other two legs. Note where each line intersects the overlapping lines of the body or leg.

Carefully erase "leftover" ovals before moving to the final step. If they're too dark–as in this example–you may want to start again, using what you've learned to make the second drawing even better.

5. Because the addax is light colored, you don't need to shade the whole body. Make your pencil strokes get lighter toward highlight areas. In the lightest areas, you don't need to shade at all.

Starting with the darkest areas of the body, add light, short pencil strokes for fur. Leave the belly and side lighter.

Clean up any smudges with your eraser. Put today's date on your drawing and save it in your portfolio!

Arabian Oryx

Oryx leucoryx

SE Saudi Arabia.
Size: 2 m (6½ ft) long

The only oryx found outside Africa, this small, rare animal travels widely in extreme desert conditions to find grass and shrubs to eat. It shelters from the sun by scraping a hollow under a bush or on the side of a sand dune. This oryx has been over hunted for its hide, meat and horns. Protected by law, it may be extinct in the wild (the last wild one seen was in 1972). It lives in captivity, though, and hopefully can be reintroduced to its native habitat.

ALWAYS SKETCH LIGHTLY AT FIRST!

1. This drawing starts out with three ovals tilting in all different directions. The tilt of the ovals will capture the way the animal stands, or moves. The ovals also remind you of the underlying anatomy as you draw. Draw the ovals.

2. Notice the height of the head in relation to the shoulder (just a little bit above). Make a light circle for the head, a smaller one for the nose, and lines to connect them. Add the eye, halfway up the head circle and off to the left. Draw the ears. Draw a line to connect the head with the top of the body, and continue your line along the top—connecting all body ovals. Add the swishing tail. Draw the bottom of the neck.

3. Starting with small circles for the joints, draw the two closest legs. Note the angles of the rear leg.

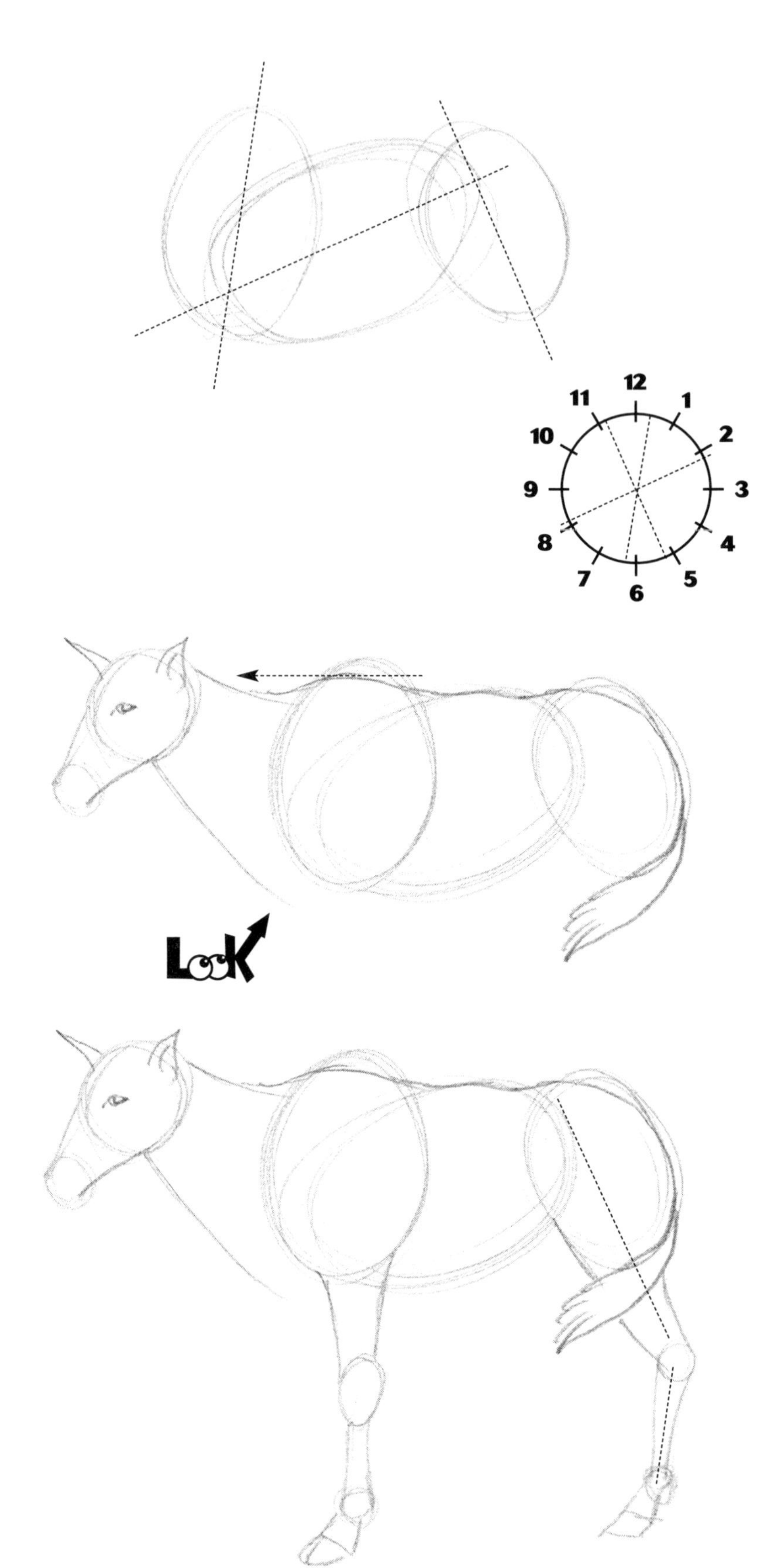

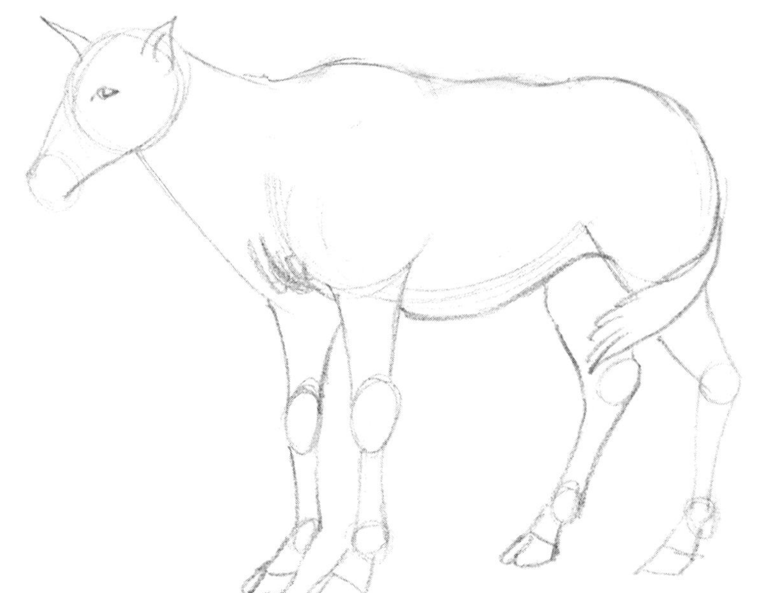

4. Starting with light circles for the joints, draw the other two legs. Notice how the bottom of the neck meets the front leg. Connect the belly and the rear leg.

5. Draw the long, curved horns–lightly at first *(of course!).*

A couple of hints:

When drawing the horns, turn the paper so that the curve comes naturally. If you're left handed, you may need to turn your paper sideways to make the curve comfortable.

To keep from smudging, place a piece of clean paper over the part you've already drawn. Rest the heel of your hand on this. Keep the paper still, or it might smudge the drawing underneath.

Add the mouth and nose. Carefully shade the face to make the facial patterns.

6. Using short pencil strokes, continue shading the body. Pay attention to the direction of the lines and their darkness. Leave the belly light. Darken the hooves and add a little bit of grass. Make a couple of lines for distant sand dunes behind the oryx.

Orsome Oryx! Clean up any smudges with your eraser, put today's date on your drawing and save it in your portfolio!

Arabian Toad-Headed Agamid

Phrynocephalus nejdensis

SW Asia. Size: up to 12.5 cm (5 in)

This burrowing lizard digs short tunnels for shelter. It can also bury itself in sand by wriggling from side to side. It eats mainly insects but also some flowers and leaves. If alarmed, it will stand high on its legs, and roll and unroll its tail; this is its defensive posture.

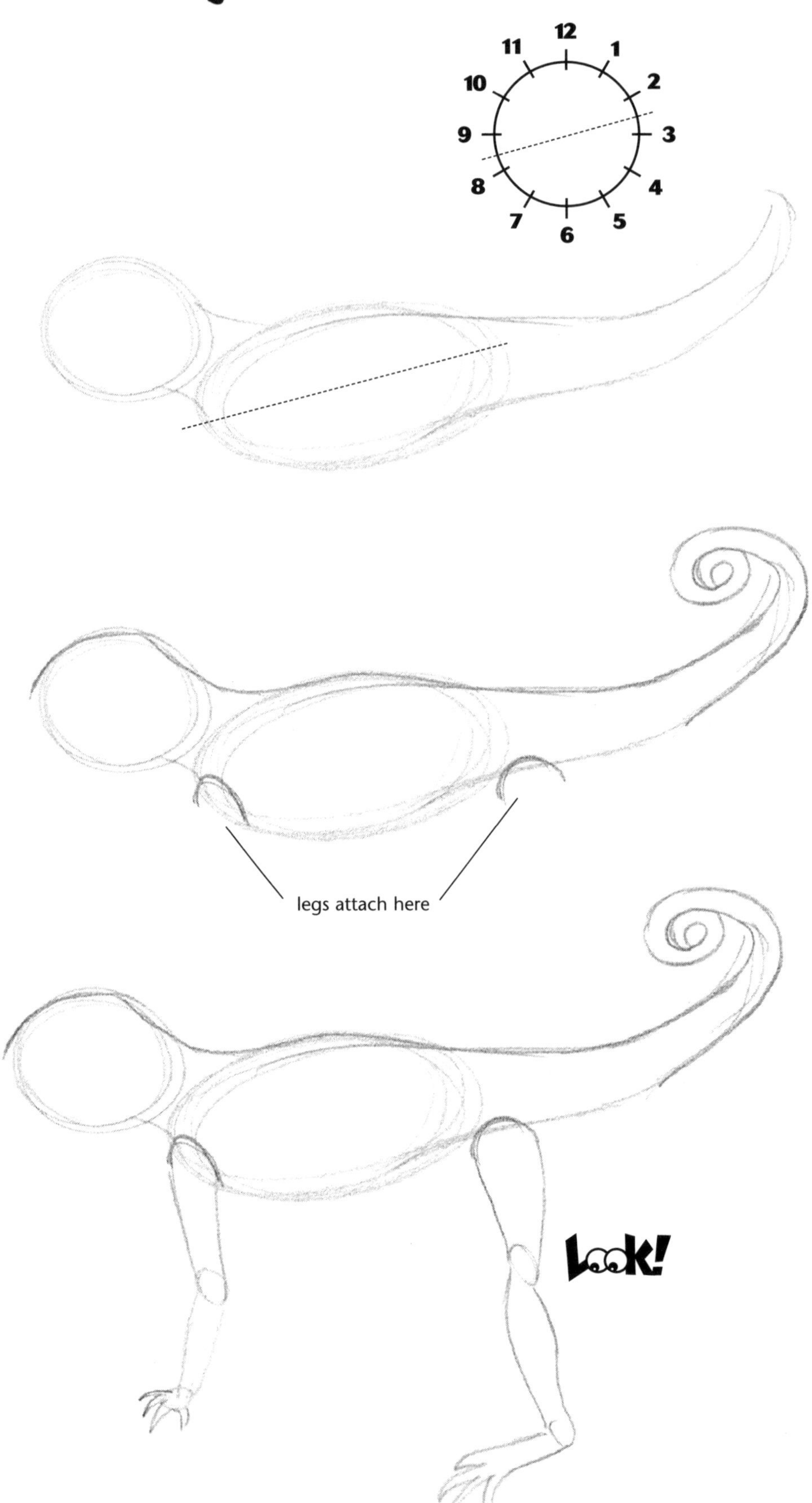

1. Begin your drawing by lightly sketching the tilted horizontal oval of the body. Compare the tilt of the oval to the clock face: this forward angle helps convey the defensive posture. To the oval, add gently curving lines for the tail. At the other end, draw a rounder oval for the head, and connect it to the body with two short lines for the neck.

2. Draw one smooth line over the top of the head, neck, and back, connecting the ovals and the tail. Draw small curves to locate the attachment points for the legs. Carefully add the spiralling tip of the tail.

3. As always when drawing limbs, use small, light circles to mark the joints. Add curved lines to finish the legs. Notice the distinct curves in the rear leg. Draw the feet.

Refine the details before adding shading and finishing touches.

4. Draw the tilted eye with its thick eyebrow above. Add the mouth, swooping down and back into the jaw line. Draw the small visible parts of the two legs on the far side of the lizard. Refine the bottom of the neck, belly, and tail, adding the curved flaps just behind the rear leg.

If your drawing looks good to you, continue. Otherwise, save it as a practice sketch, putting it in your portfolio with today's date.

5. To complete our friend the toad head, lightly outline the stripes on the legs and tail, and the spots on the back. Carefully shade from one end to the other and back again, looking for any details you missed. Add the *cast shadow* beneath.

   Go over the outline with a sharpened pencil. Clean up any smudges with your eraser.

Toadally cool, dude! Put today's date on your drawing and save it in your portfolio!

Bactrian camel

Camelus ferus

Central Asia, Northern Africa, Middle East. Size: 3m (10) long, 2m (7 ft) high at shoulder

Bactrian camels have two humps–think of the letter B turned on its side. The humps store fat to help them survive when food is scarce. They eat grass, and foliage of bushes and trees. Their long, shaggy hair keeps them warm in the winter, but they shed it in the summer. They move slowly with a rolling gait, able to lift two legs on the same side at the same time.

1. Start out by lightly sketching the large, slightly tilted oval of the body. *Intersecting* it, draw the small, narrow oval of the hip. Notice how it tilts. Add a U shape for the shaggy front leg, dropping down below the body.

2. Add two humps on the back. Sketch a circle for the head. Where does it lie in relation to the first oval you drew? Add a short line connecting it to the back, and draw a long, shaggy, U shape for the neck. Draw the tail.

3. Three-fourths of the way up the head, draw a horizontal line. Fill in, above the line, with spiked hair. *(Nice hair!)*. Halfway up the head, draw an ear on either side. Level with the top of the ears, draw the nostrils. Level with the bottom of the ears, draw the top of the mouth. Add more lines on the nose and mouth.

   Draw the eyes between the nostrils and ears, and use short pencil strokes to make the shaggy hair on the face and neck.

ALWAYS SKETCH LIGHTLY AT FIRST!

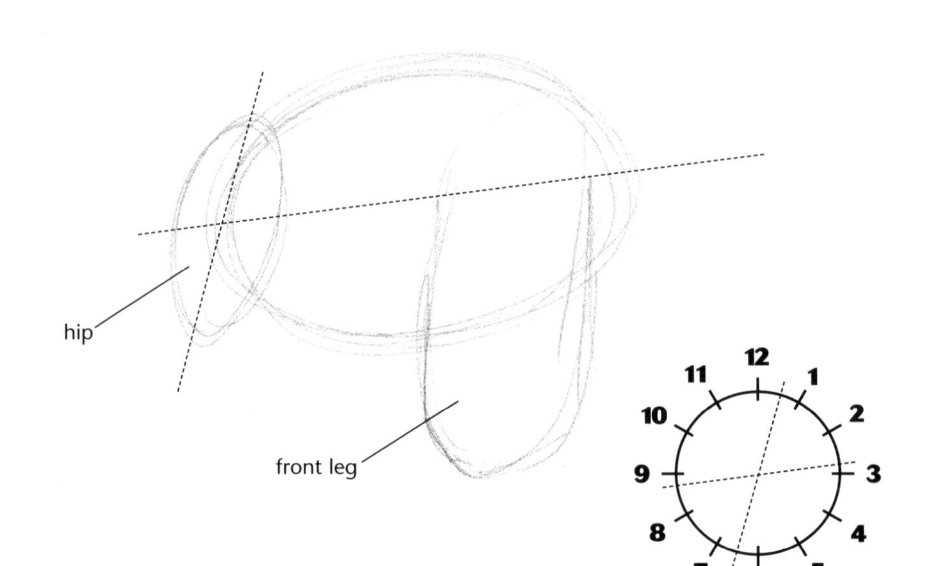

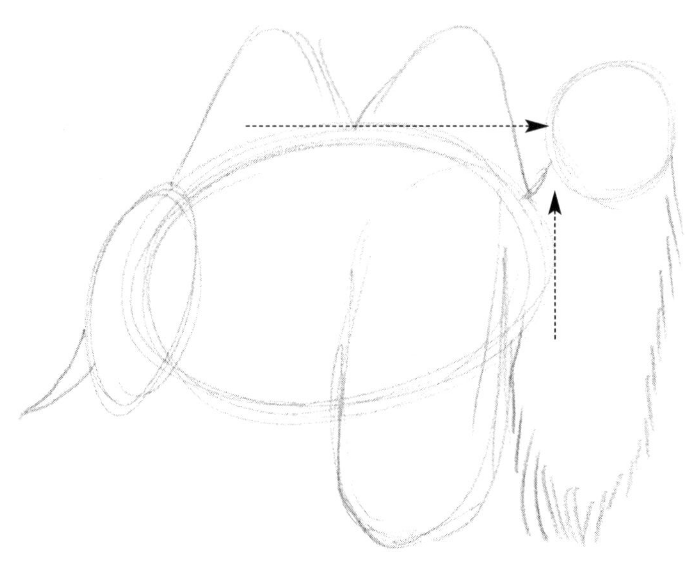

Where does the head lie in relation to the first oval you drew?

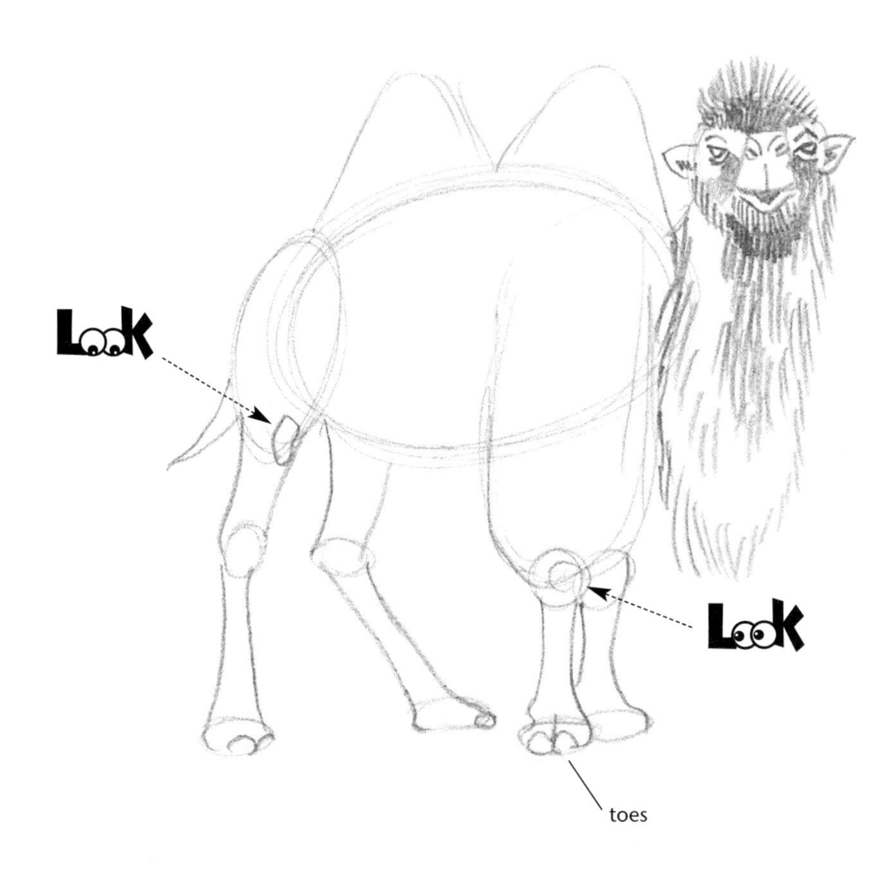

4. At the bottom of the front leg U, draw small ovals for the leg joints. Draw wide, low ovals for the hooves, and curving lines connecting them to the top part of the leg. Notice how one leg overlaps part of the other. Add toes.

   Using similar ovals and lines, complete the rear legs. Add the tail.

   Look: *where the camel kneels, thick callus builds up on the legs. On your body, the calluses on the rear leg would be on your knees; the ones in front on the back of your wrists.*

5. Finish your drawing by carefully adding short pencil strokes to shade the body and add texture.

   Take your time. Which parts are darkest? Which are lightest? What direction do the lines run on each part of the body? You'll improve quickly if you get in the habit of asking these questions often as you draw.

   Add a small *cast shadow* under the camel. Clean up any smudges with your eraser.

   Oh, by the way, camels spit. Does your camel look like it's spitting at you? Whether or not, put today's date on your drawing and save it in your portfolio!

Camel spider (Wind scorpion)

Solifugida, or *Solipugida*

Africa, Orient, America, Southern Spain. Size: up to 15 cm (6 in) span across outstretched legs

These hairy, fast-moving *arachnids* (spider relatives) hunt for insects at night, sometimes eating lizards, small mammals and birds. They have strong *chelicerae* (that's what an arachnid's "jaws" are called), with which they chop, squash and chew the victim, which ends up a formless lump. They may move as fast as 16 km/h (10 mph). Also known as wind scorpions or sun spiders, they like the drier parts of the desert and stay away from oases.

Yikes! This one looks complicated! Start with the simplest shapes, and add one piece at a time...

1. Sketch the two main body parts: one long and bullet-shaped; the other almost a circle.

2. Add two dots for eyes. Draw the huge jaw on the closer side of the head, and the little bit of jaw visible on the other side.

3. Just behind the jaw, add the first segment of the first *pedipalp* (feeler: like legs but without claws), then the next segment.

4. Add remaining segments, and four visible segments of the other pedipalp.

5. Draw the second set of feeler legs. Notice how they go *under* the first set, adding *depth* to your drawing **(look)**.

6. The third set of legs supports the spider. These walking legs go straight out to the side. Draw them thicker, and stronger.

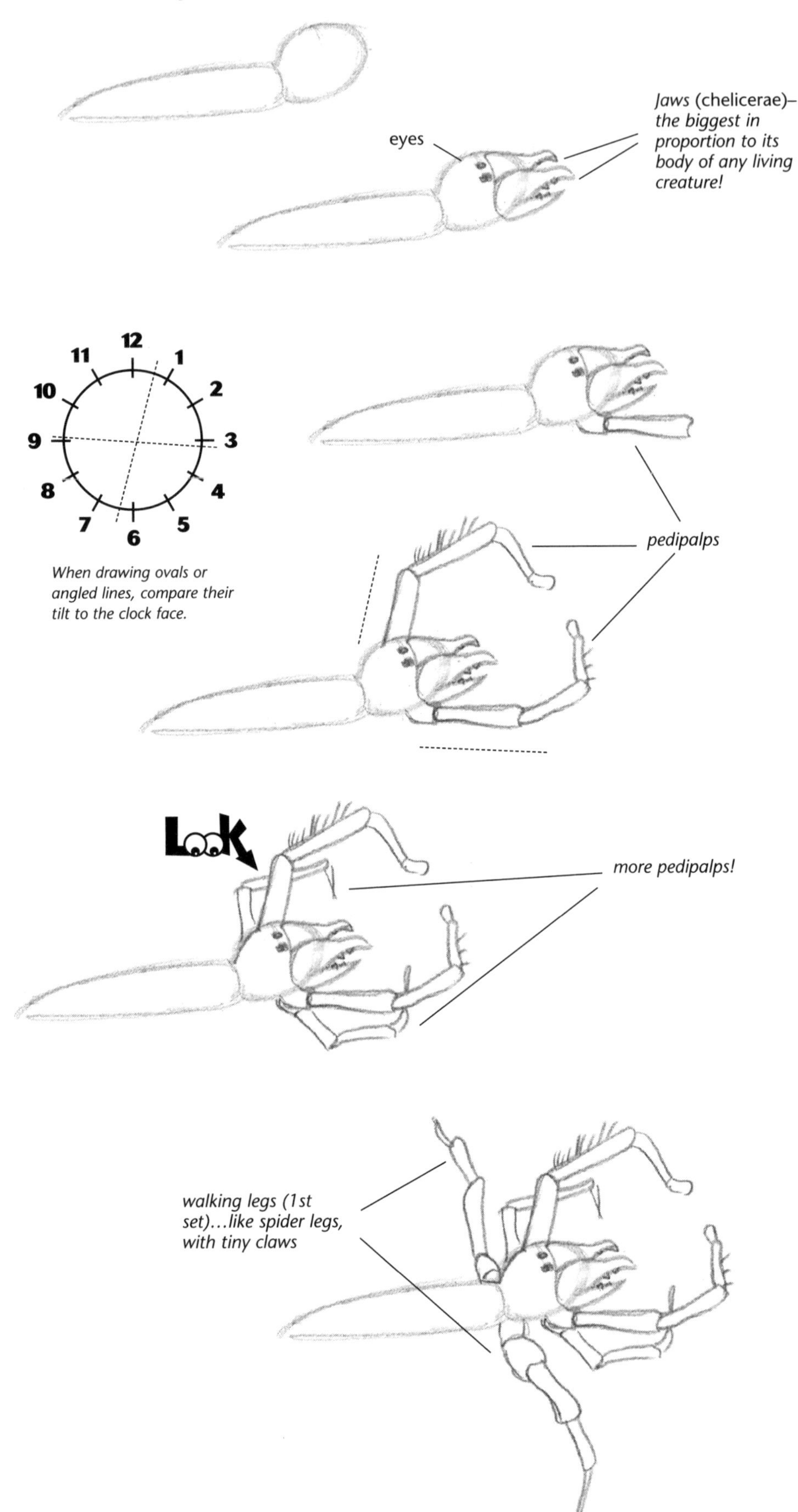

When drawing ovals or angled lines, compare their tilt to the clock face.

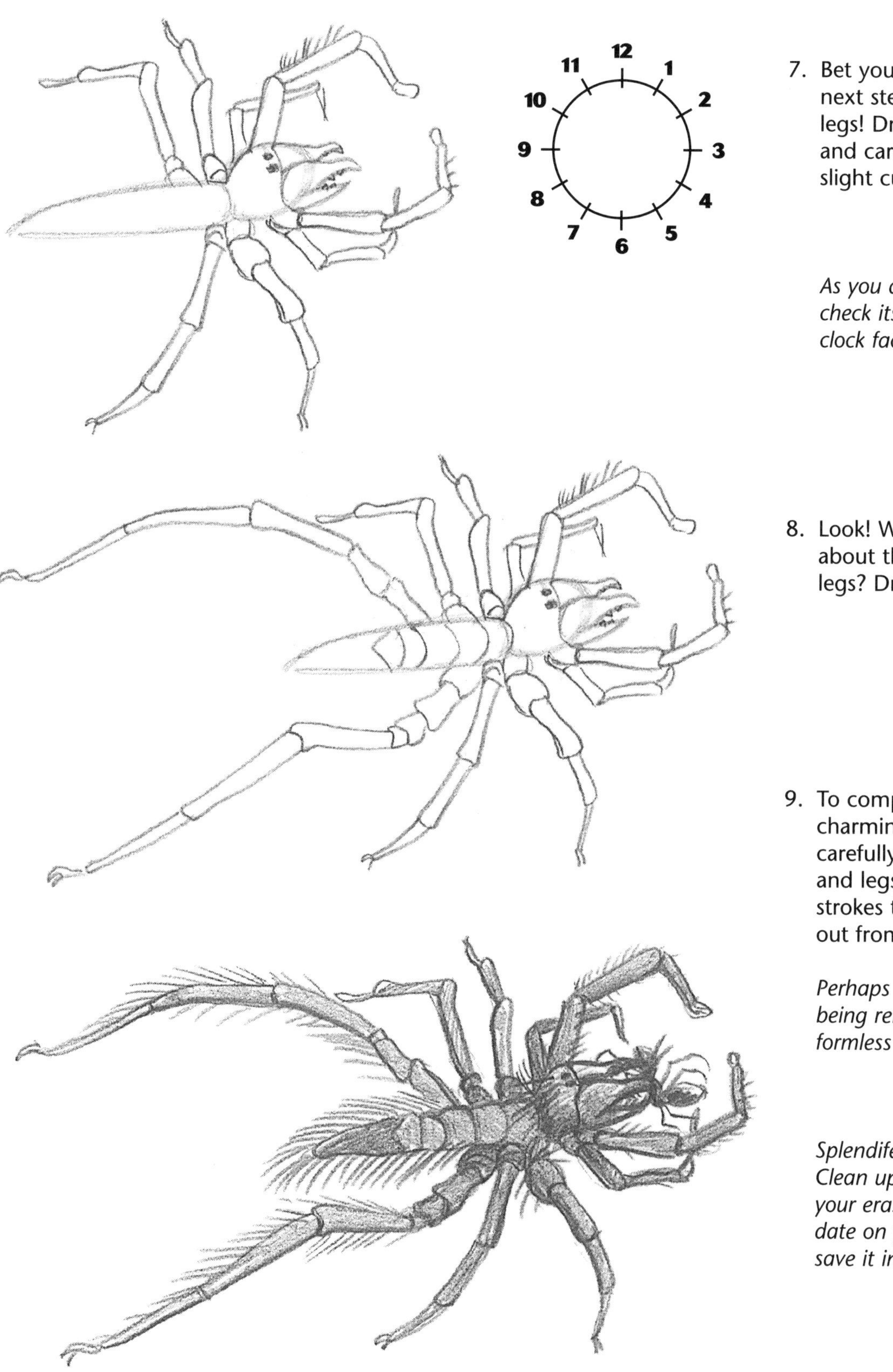

7. Bet you can't guess the next step: another set of legs! Draw them slowly and carefully. Notice the slight curves and angles.

As you draw each segment, check its angle against the clock face.

8. Look! What's different about the last set of legs? Draw them!

9. To complete this charming character, carefully shade the body and legs. Use short pencil strokes to make the hairs, out from the body.

Perhaps add a hapless ant, being rendered into a formless lump...

Splendiferous arachnid! Clean up any smudges with your eraser, put today's date on your drawing and save it in your portfolio!

Caracal

Felis caracal

Africa, Middle East to India.
Size: .8 – 1.2 m (33 – 47 in) including tail

The solitary caracal patrols a home range, preying on mammals from mice to medium sized antelopes, including birds, reptiles, and smaller domestic animals. Females bear litters of 2-3 young, who don't become independent until they've reached the age of 9-12 months.

1. Before you draw, **look** at how much room divides the two ovals of the cat's body. Now sketch one round oval; make the other narrower and slightly tilted. Add the curving lines for the top and bottom of the body.

2. Sketch a small circle for the head, level with the top of the shoulder. Draw the ears with their tufts of hair at the end. Connect the head to the body with short, curved neck lines. Sketch a smaller circle for the nose.

3. In the upper right of the small nose circle, draw the dark triangle of the nose, with whiskers sticking out either side. **Look** at the difference between the two eyes. Add a line curving up and back, with the round eye underneath. Draw the small visible bit of the other eye.

4. Sketch small circles to locate the joints on the back leg. Draw the leg, paying careful attention to the angle of each section.

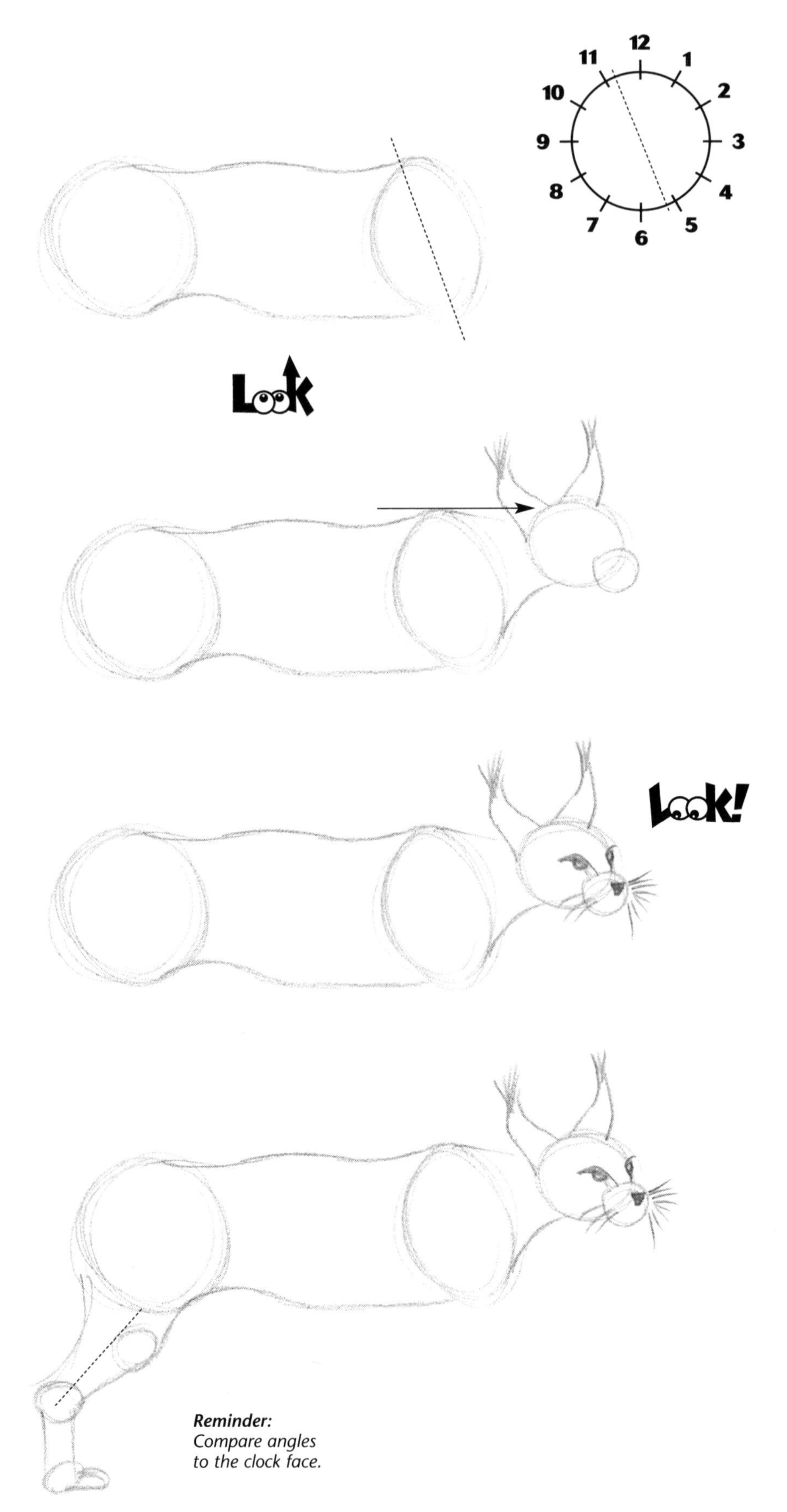

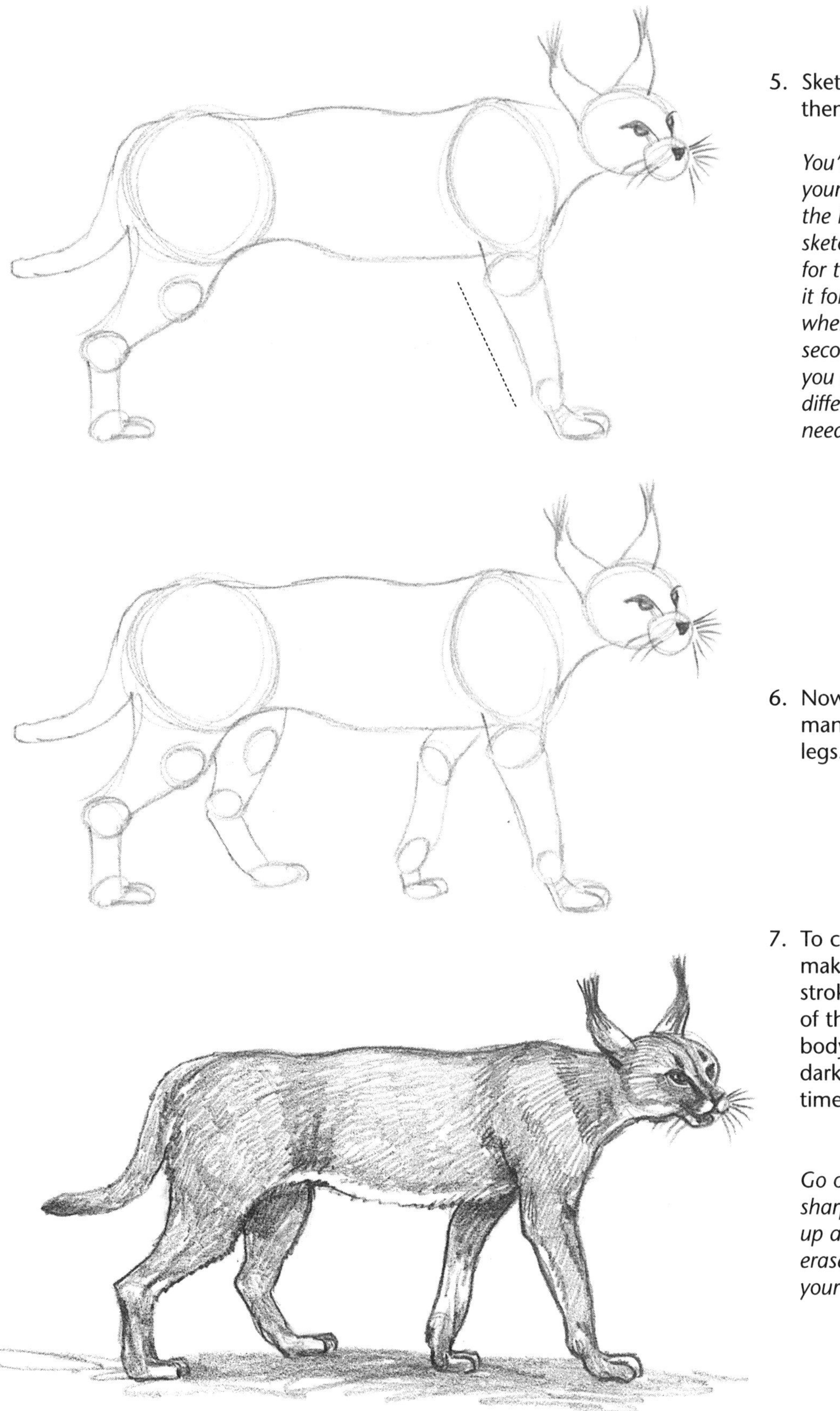

5. Sketch the front leg ovals, then draw the front leg.

   You'll find it very helpful in your drawing if you get in the habit of lightly sketching those little circles for the joints. For one thing, it forces you to figure out where the limb bends. A second reason: it also helps you draw the limbs in different positions if you need to.

6. Now, in a similar manner, add the other legs.

7. To complete the caracal, make short pencil strokes—in the direction of the fur—over the entire body. Note lighter and darker areas. Take your time.

   Go over the outline with a sharpened pencil, and clean up any smudges with your eraser. Put today's date on your drawing and save it!

Desert Cottontail

ALWAYS SKETCH LIGHTLY AT FIRST!

Sylvilagus auduboni

North America.
Size: 35 — 45 cm (9-11 in) incl. tail

Desert cottontails make their shelter in a burrow or shallow depression in the ground. Most active in the late afternoon and evening, they stay close to cover, When alarmed, they dart away quickly, flicking up their tails as they run, showing the white underside. The young are born blind and helpless after a gestation period of 26-30 days.

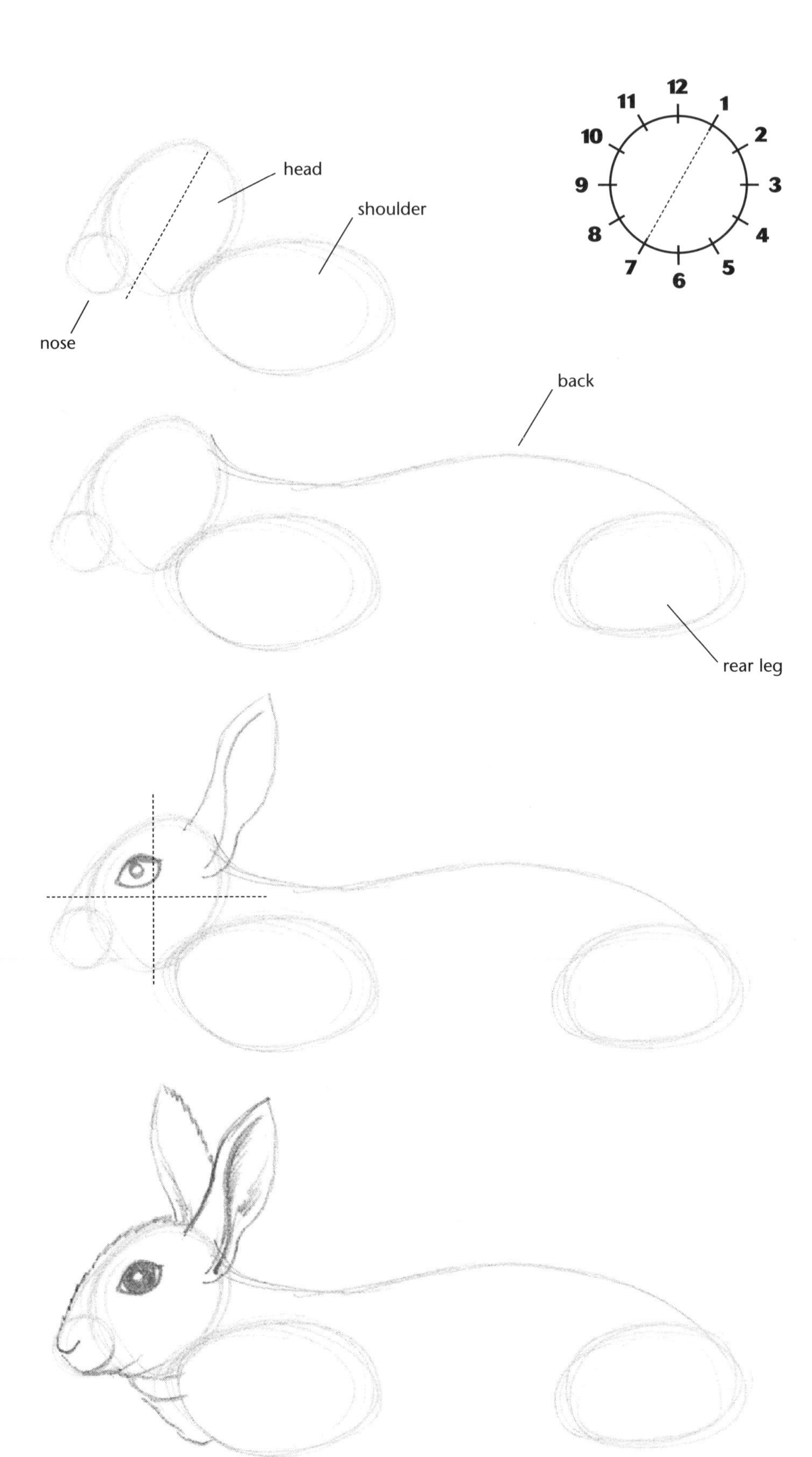

1. Sketch a horizontal oval for the rabbit's shoulder, and a tilted oval for the head. Sketch a small circle for the nose and connect it to the head with lines.

2. Sketch another horizontal oval to begin the rear leg. Connect it to the head with the long, swooping line of the back.

3. Notice where the eye appears in the head. Draw the eye with a circle for the highlight. Add the ear. Make it about as long as the rest of the head.

4. Draw the second ear. Darken the eye (except for the small circle). Add lines for the nostril and mouth, and lines for the chin and throat.

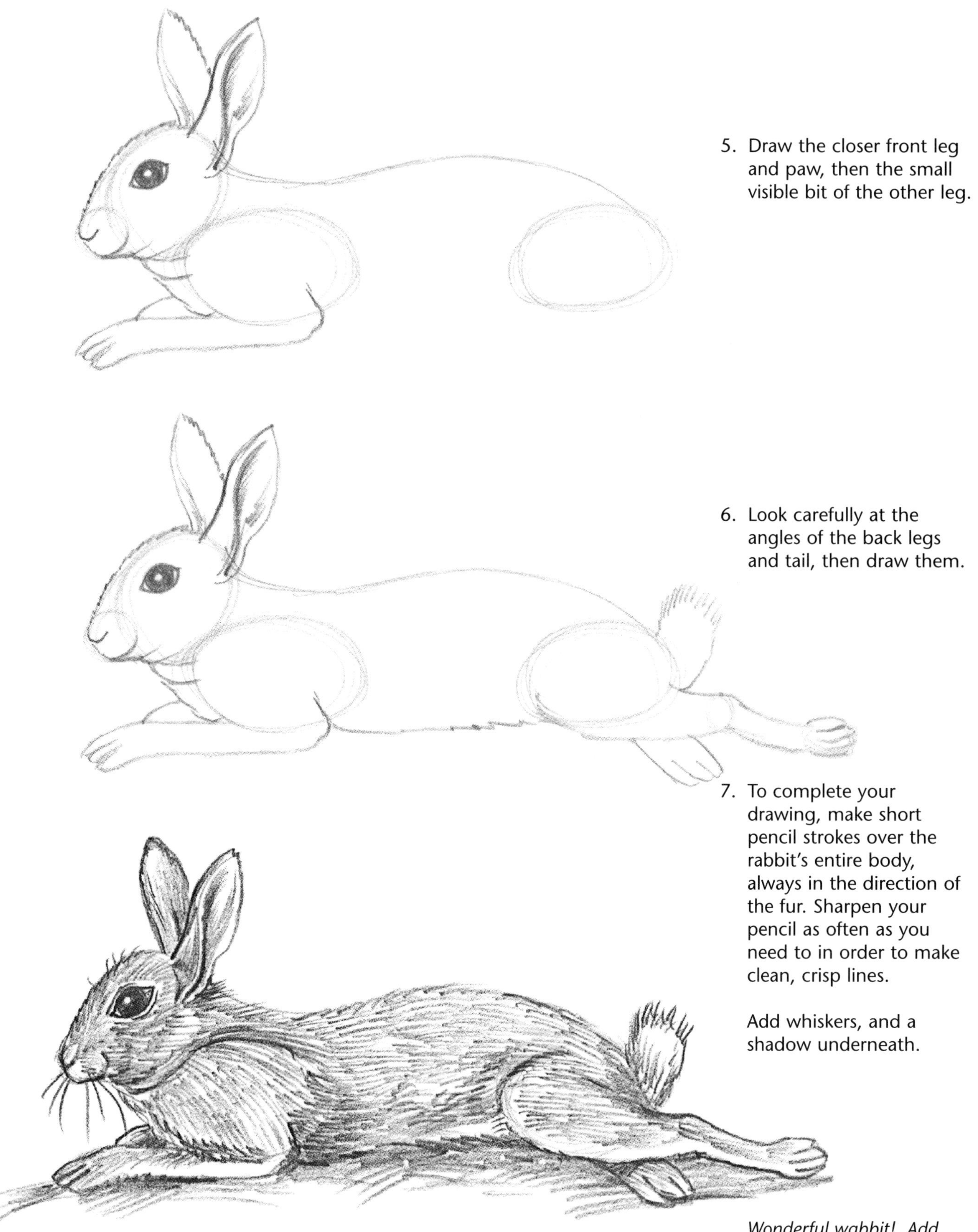

5. Draw the closer front leg and paw, then the small visible bit of the other leg.

6. Look carefully at the angles of the back legs and tail, then draw them.

7. To complete your drawing, make short pencil strokes over the rabbit's entire body, always in the direction of the fur. Sharpen your pencil as often as you need to in order to make clean, crisp lines.

   Add whiskers, and a shadow underneath.

Wonderful wabbit! Add today's date and save your drawing!

Desert Tortoise

ALWAYS SKETCH LIGHTLY AT FIRST!

Gopherus agassizi

SW United States.
Size: up to 51 cm (20 in) long

During the heat of the day, the desert tortoise stays in an underground burrow, which may be up to 9 M (30 ft) long. It gets all its water from plants it eats, such as cactus and succulents. A desert tortoise can exist an entire dry season without water!

Look

1. Sketch an upward arc and a downward arc for the top and bottom of the shell. Note the straight section at the neck.

2. Lightly sketch the front and rear legs, and the lower part of the shell, including the point behind the rear leg.

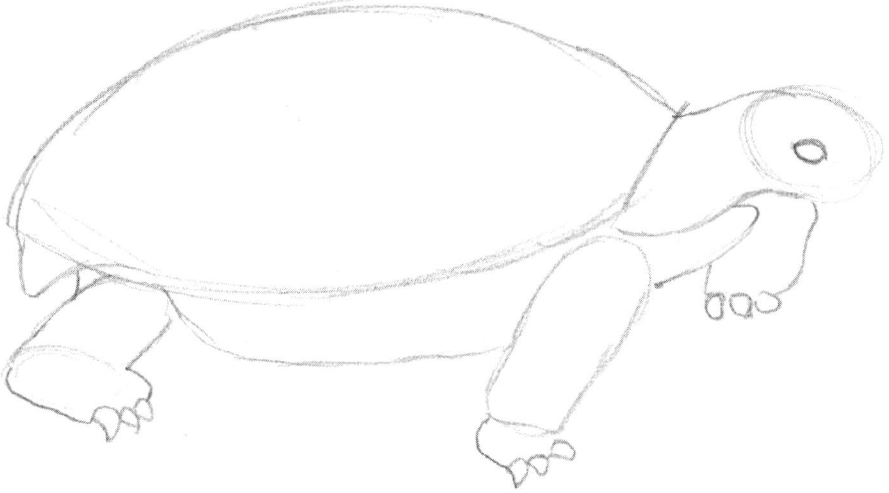

3. Sketch an oval for the head. Add the neck, eye, and the part of the shell underneath the head, and the visible portion of the other front leg. Draw the feet. Don't forget claws!

4. Carefully lay out the row of hexagons (six-sided shapes) on the top of the shell.

ALWAYS SKETCH LIGHTLY AT FIRST!

5. Continue laying out the hexagon pattern on top of the shell, above the row of hexagons, and the rectangle shapes on the bottom of the shell.

6. Shade the bottom part of the shell. Add shadows to create the folds on the neck. Darken the eye, leaving a small white area. Draw small scaly patterns on the head, front leg, and feet.

7. Light and dark contrasts make the tortoise drawing come to life. Look at the dark areas; see which areas stay light.

Add lots and lots and lots of small lines in the patterns of the shell–some lighter, some darker. Add more small scaly patterns on the head, neck, legs and feet.

Draw a shadow on the ground, and a few small marks for pebbles.

Torrific tortoise! Clean up any smudges with your eraser, put today's date on your drawing and save it in your portfolio!

Diamondback Rattlesnake

ALWAYS SKETCH LIGHTLY AT FIRST!

Crotalus atrox

Southwest US & northern Mexico.
Size: .76 – 2.25 m (2½ – 7½ ft)

The markings on the western diamondback aren't as distinct as you'd think from the name: on the back you'll see diamond-shaped or hexagonal markings, but you may have to look carefully *(and by the time you get that close, the snake is probably rattling its tail at you in warning!).* Overall, the snake has a speckled or dusty appearance. The tail is set off by broad black and white rings. When rattlesnakes strike, their fangs pierce the victim just for a split second, enough time to inject poison. Then they retreat to their hiding place. Later they look for their kill.

Have fun with this drawing. Enjoy practicing the swooping curves!

1. Sketch gentle, curving lines for the top and bottom of the snake's body. Join them in an upward curve for the fang, and add an extending lower jaw.

2. Look at the rear portion—then carefully draw it. Add the other fang, and mouth details.

3. Extend the body downward. Study how each line curves. Two of them even run into each other **(look)**.

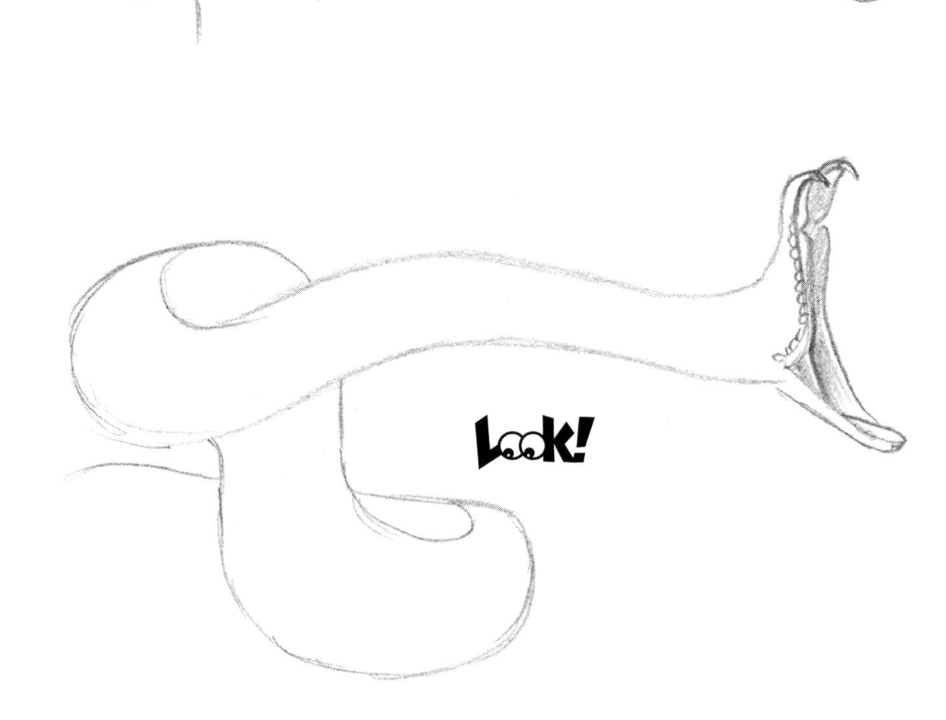

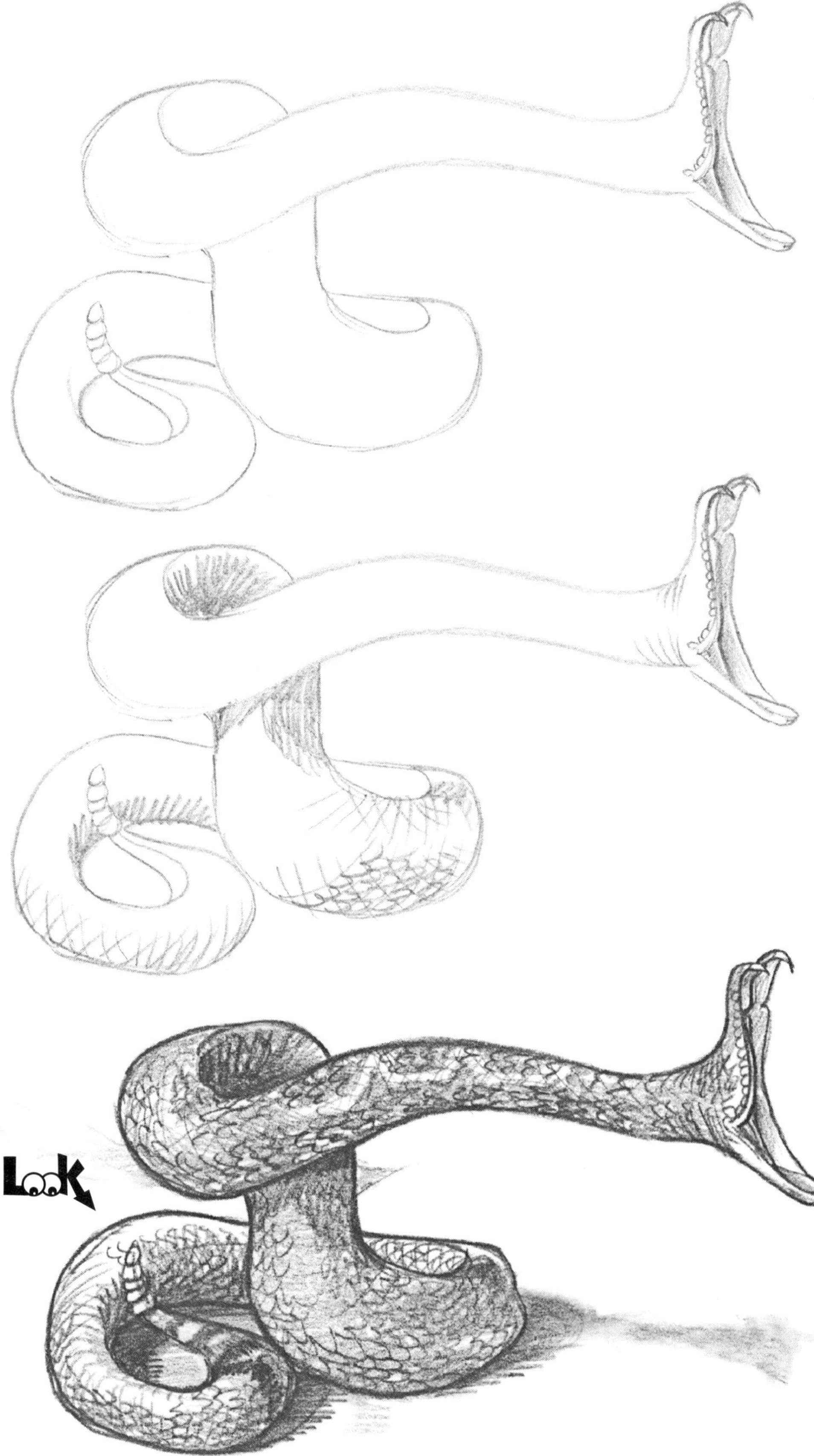

4. Draw curving lines to finish the body and the tail. Draw small ovals for the rattles.

Before you go on, look at your drawing. Is your snake shape smooth and flowing? If not, try again, practicing nice, smooth, connecting curves. Get comfortable with drawing the snake before you spend time adding scales and shading. Save your sketches (with today's date!) in your portfolio!

5. Add *crosshatching* (crisscrossing lines), curving around the *contour* to create guide lines for scales. Use short pencil strokes to darken the shadows.

6. Shade the whole body—except, of course, for highlights **(look)** and the faint pattern on the back. Continue shading and adding scales. Go over the outline with a sharpened pencil. Add the distinct light and dark bands on the tail.

Draw a *cast shadow* on the ground. Soften it by rubbing it with your finger or a piece of paper.

Clean up any smudges with your eraser. Put today's date on your drawing and save it in your portfolio!

Dromedary

Camelus dromedarius

North Africa, Middle East.
Size: body 2.2 – 3.4 m (7¼ – 11 ft);
tail 50 cm (19¾ in)

Not a wild animal! People who know think the one-humped camel has been domesticated since 4,000 BC. Today, you'll find two types: heavy, slow-moving beasts of burden, and graceful, fast racers used for riding. They feed on grass and other available plants, and can withstand long periods in areas of tough, sparse vegetation without drinking, thanks to adaptations in their stomach linings and kidneys. In one experiment, a thirsty camel drank 104 liters (27 US gallons) of water in ten minutes! The hump stores fat, not water. Females breed every other year. The long gestation period (365-440 days) results in a single young that can walk after a day.

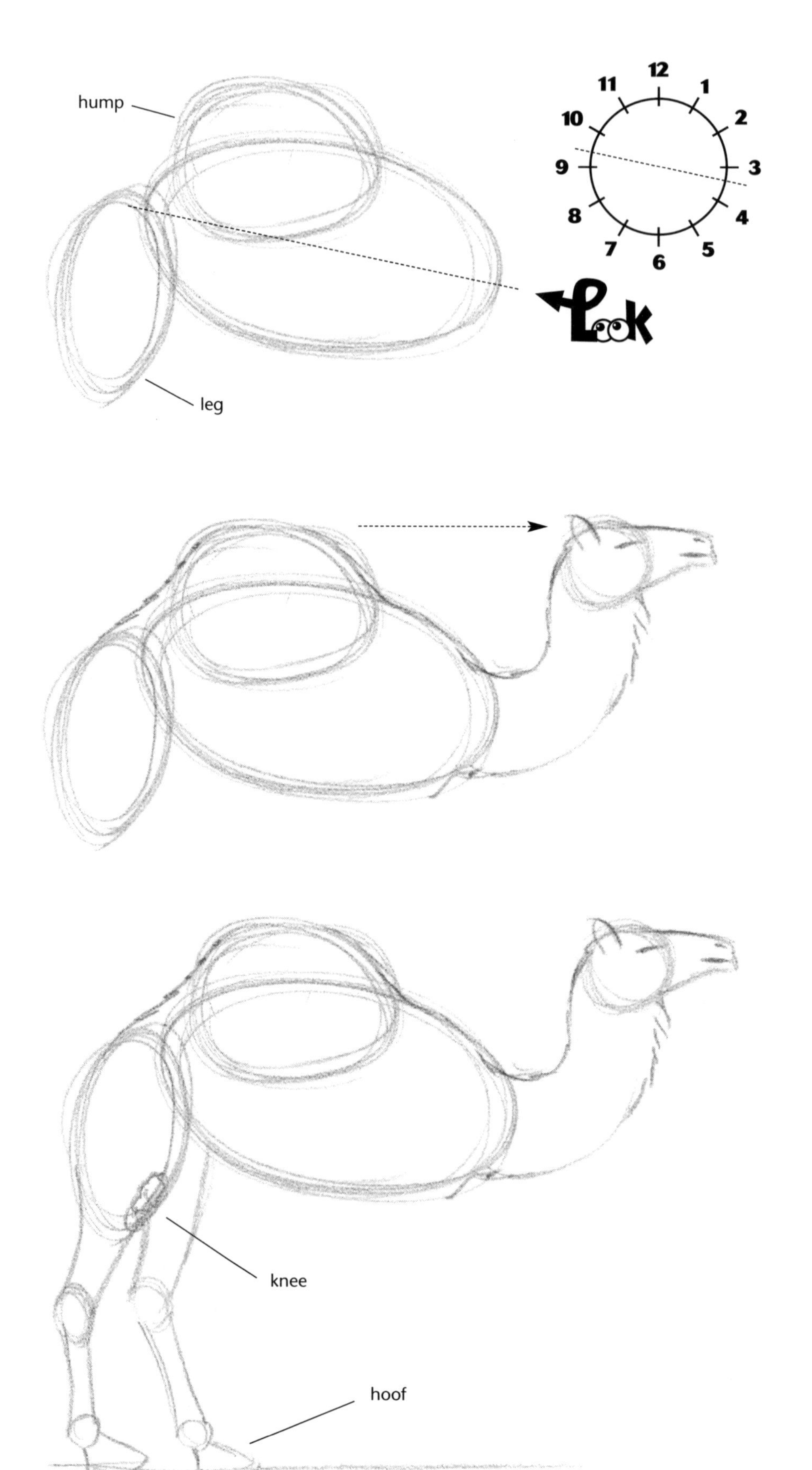

1. Sketch a large, slightly tilted, oval. Sketch a smaller oval, off-center, for the hump. Add a vertical oval for the rear leg.

2. Level with the top of the hump, sketch a small circle for the head. Add lines to form the front of the head. Draw the mouth and nostril. Add the eye and the ear. Draw the gently curving (and slightly shaggy) lines for the neck.

3. Draw the callused knee at the bottom front of the leg oval. Sketch circles for the leg joints. Add curving lines to complete the rear legs. Draw wide, almost triangular shapes for the camel's spreading hoofs.

4. Next, add the front legs. Notice the callus on the front of the front leg. The callused areas on the front and rear legs are from kneeling, to lie down and get up again.

   A camel folds its legs underneath to reduce exposure to the hot desert sun (see sketch of Bactrian camels on page 62.). *Also, the camel's food store–the fat-filled hump on its back–helps insulate the body underneath from the sun's heat.*

5. Using your eraser, carefully clean up sketch lines you no longer need.

   Add pencil strokes—always in the direction of the hair and contours of the body—to shade *just* the shadow areas.

   Go over the outline with a sharpened pencil. Add a *cast shadow* beneath, and *(why not?)* a couple of pyramids in the distance.

   Dazzling dromedary! Clean up any smudges with your eraser, put today's date on your drawing and save it in your portfolio!

Egyptian Slit-Faced Bat

ALWAYS SKETCH LIGHTLY AT FIRST!

Nycteris thebaica

Middle East, Africa south of Sahara.
Size: body 4.5 – 7.5 cm (1¾ – 3 in);
wingspan 16 – 28 cm (6¼ – 11 in)

Hang around ancient Egyptian temples, and you just may run into a few of these! Slit-faced bats like to catch a variety of invertebrates for supper. Scorpions seem to be a favorite! The bats usually give birth to a single young in January or February; they may do the same later in the year.

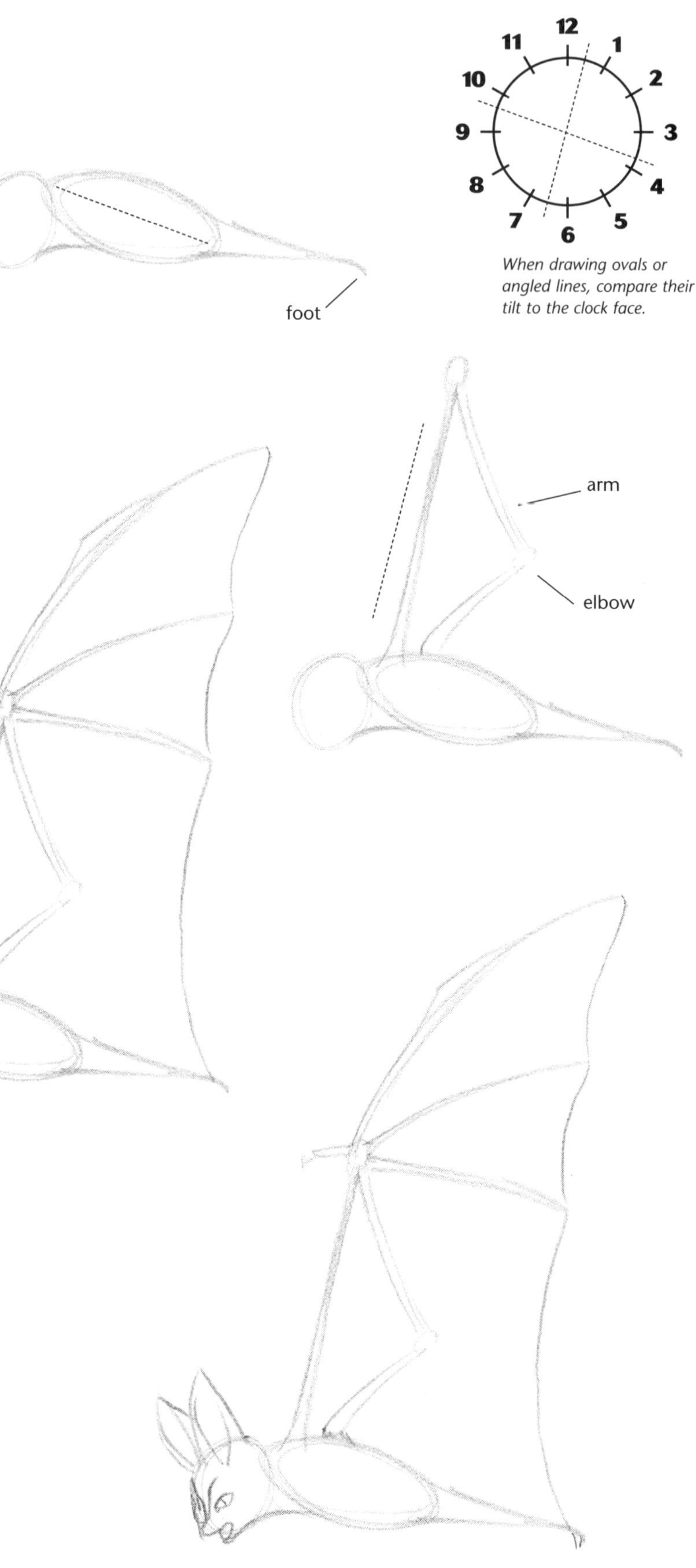

When drawing ovals or angled lines, compare their tilt to the clock face.

1. Sketch a flat, slightly tilted oval for the bat's body. Sketch a circle at one end for the head. Add a neck line to connect it to the body. Draw two lines tapering to the foot.

2. Draw the front of the wing, up from the top of the body (compare the angle with the clock face). Sketch tiny circles and lines for the bent arm holding it out.

3. From the point where the arm and wing lines meet, draw the bat's long thin "fingers" spreading out to make triangular shapes. Draw the back edge of the wing, connecting it to the tapered end of the foot.

4. Look closely at the bat's facial features—mouth, nose, the little sensing organ on top of the nose, eyes and eye slits. Add them. Draw the ears.

   These facial features are part of their "radar," picking up signals, making it possible for them to move and hunt with precision.

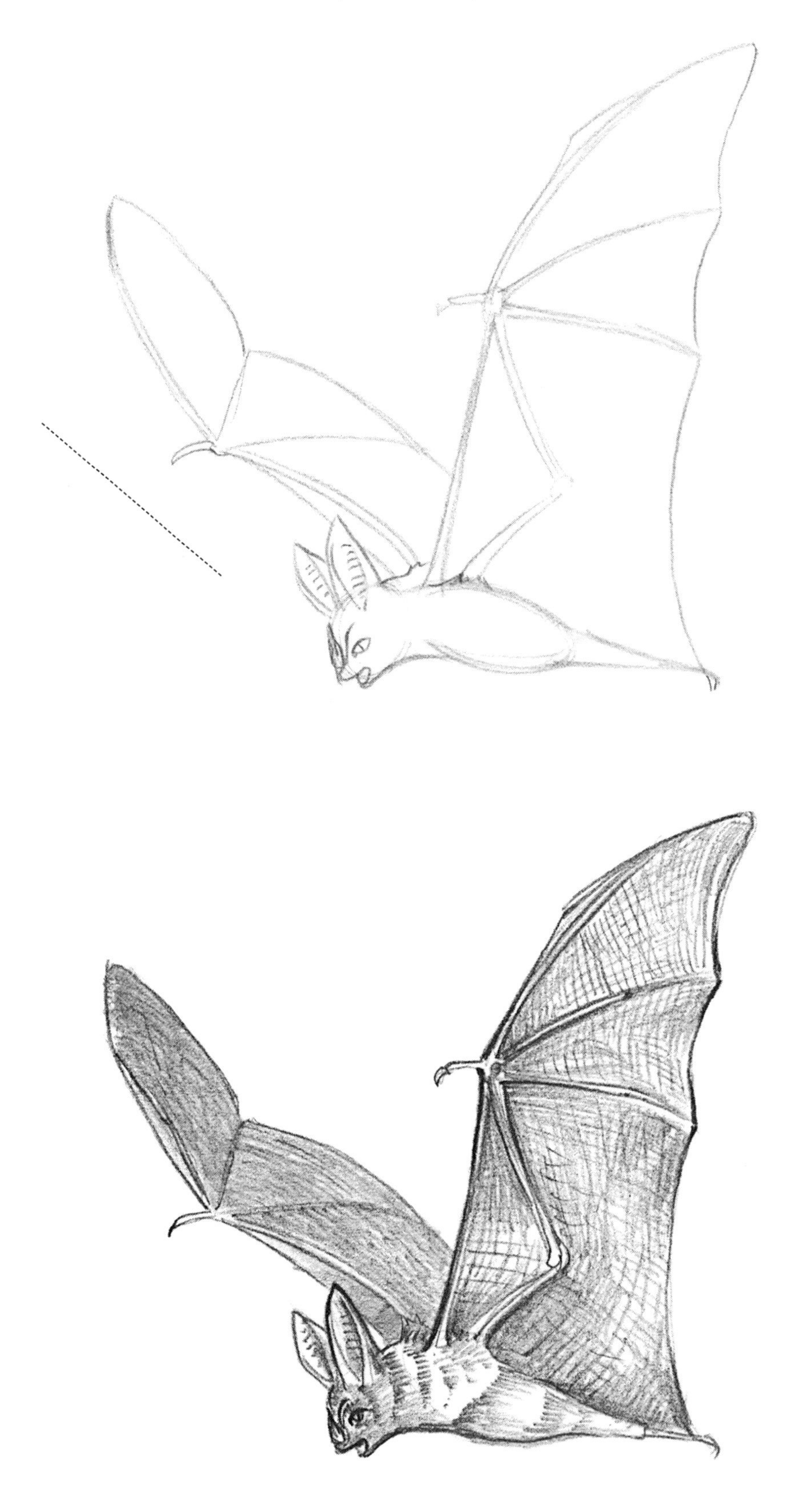

5. Add small lines inside the ears. Behind them, draw a slight hump in the back where the other wing attaches. Look at the wing angles. Draw the second wing.

6. Look at the contrast of light and dark in this final drawing.

   Use *crosshatching*, to carefully shade the closer wing. Use short pencil strokes to create the fur on the body. Continue shading, watching for light and dark areas, until you're through. Then take a sharpened pencil and go over lines you want to emphasize.

   Clean up any smudges with your eraser, put today's date on your drawing and save it in your portfolio!

Elf Owl

ALWAYS SKETCH LIGHTLY AT FIRST!

Micrathene whitneyi

Southwest US & Mexico.
Size: Body 12.5 – 15 cm (5 – 6 in)

Though one of the smallest owls in the world, the elf owl has a loud voice. It lives in wooded canyons and deserts with saguaro cactus, where it roosts in abandoned woodpecker holes. Elf owls use their feet to catch insects in flight; they also catch food on the ground, including grasshoppers and scorpions (they remove or crush the stinger), and sometimes small snakes and lizards.

1. Sketch a horizontal oval for the owl's head. Beneath it, add the slightly tilted vertical oval of the owl's body.

2. Toward the side of the face, draw the curved beak. On either side, draw two curved lines for eyes.

3. Darken the inside of the eyes, leaving a small refelective spot. Near the owl's right eye, draw a jagged line to show texture on the outline of the head. Add short pencil strokes, up and away from the eye, to shade the head.

4. Add more shading, with short pencil strokes, around the eyes and on the head. Draw the wing, lightly outlining the feathers.

5. Shade the wing, leaving some feather areas white. Draw short, curling strokes to create feathers on the breast and belly.

6. Look closely at the owl's legs—where they attach to the body, and the directions of each section. Draw the owl's legs. Add two lines for the branch on which the owl perches.

   Draw the tail feathers.

7. Darken the outlines of the feet and branch. Outline the wing and tail feathers. Go over your owl, top to bottom and side to side, adding feathers and shading, and making areas lighter or darker as needed.

Elf owls perch in trees and bushes when they're looking for food or resting. When it's time to nest, they find an old woodpecker hole in a cactus. Try drawing your elf owl nesting in a saguaro cactus!

Clean up any smudges with your eraser, put today's date on your drawing and save it in your portfolio!

Fat Sand Rat

ALWAYS SKETCH LIGHTLY AT FIRST!

Psammomys obesus

Algeria, east to Saudi Arabia.
Size: body 14 – 18.5 cm (5½ – 7¼ in); tail 12 – 15 cm (4¾ – 6 in)

What do you do if you can't be sure when you'll find food? If you're a fat sand rat, you lay down a thick layer of fat all over your body while food is abundant, then live off it when food is scarce. *(What other desert animals store fat?)* This gerbil is active day and night, collecting seeds and other vegetation to carry back to its burrow.

1. Sketch two light overlapping ovals for the head and face of the rat. Behind the head, sketch part of another oval—the front part of the body. Upward from that oval, sketch the rounded back curving down into the rear leg. Draw a curved line for the belly.

2. Sketch an oval for the nose and mouth. Outline the top of the head, making a smooth connection between the ovals. Just above the middle of the head, draw the eye. To the side of it, add the ear.

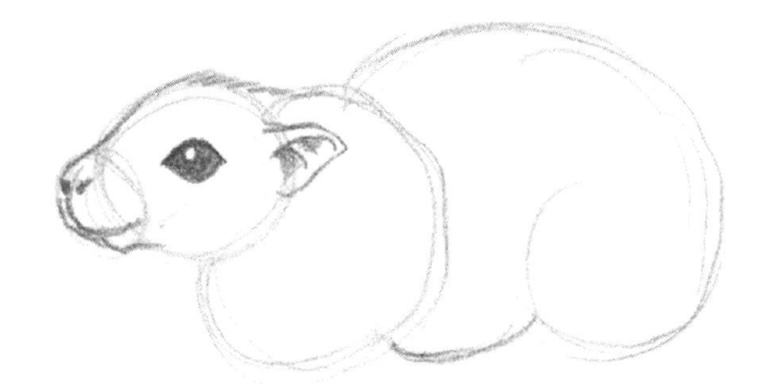

3. Darken the eye, leaving a small white reflective spot. Draw the nostrils and mouth. Outline the front of the face.

4. With a sharp pencil, draw lines above and below the eye. Add two short legs, tilting towards the front. Draw feet, then claws.

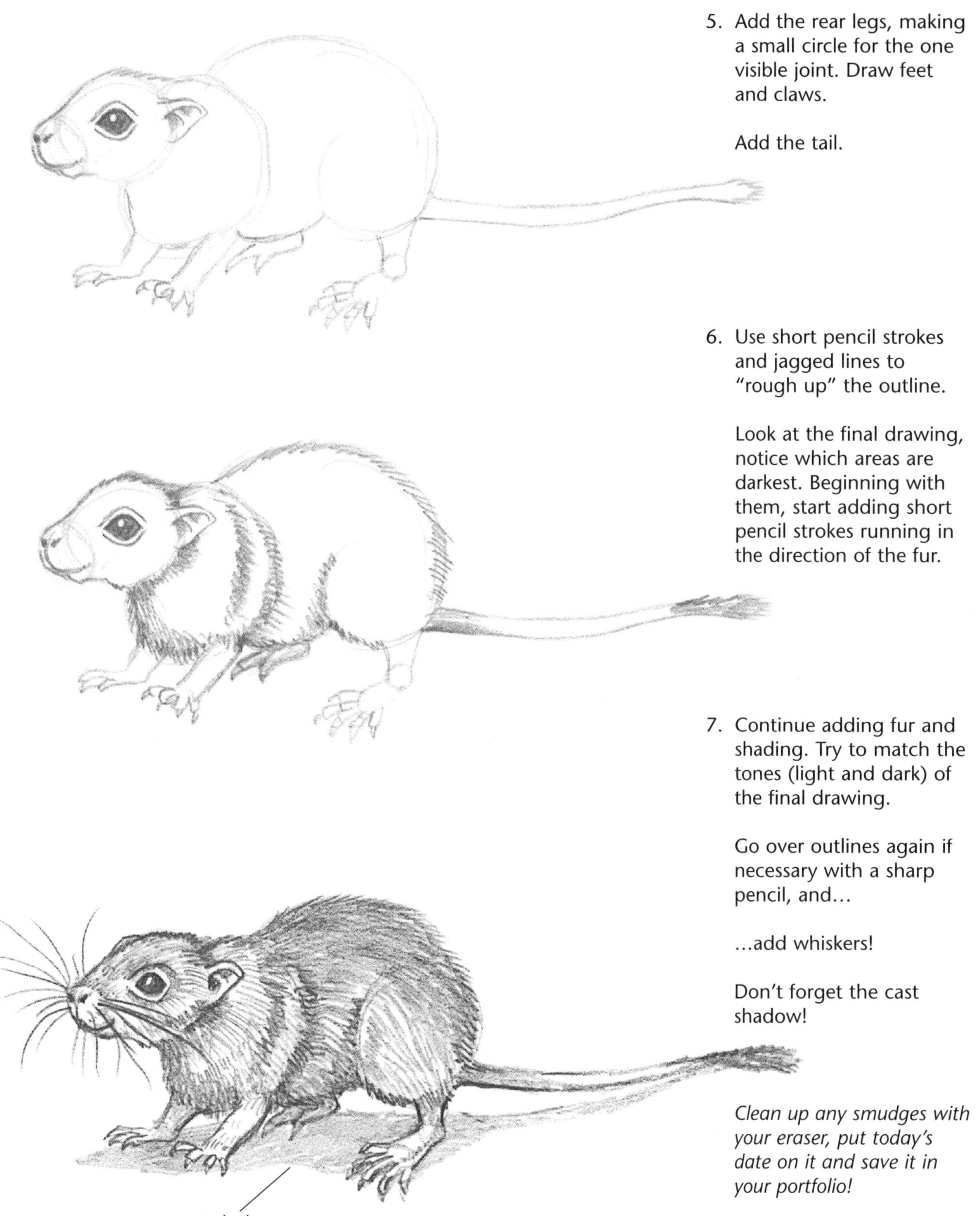

5. Add the rear legs, making a small circle for the one visible joint. Draw feet and claws.

   Add the tail.

6. Use short pencil strokes and jagged lines to "rough up" the outline.

   Look at the final drawing, notice which areas are darkest. Beginning with them, start adding short pencil strokes running in the direction of the fur.

7. Continue adding fur and shading. Try to match the tones (light and dark) of the final drawing.

   Go over outlines again if necessary with a sharp pencil, and...

   ...add whiskers!

   Don't forget the cast shadow!

Clean up any smudges with your eraser, put today's date on it and save it in your portfolio!

Fennec fox

ALWAYS SKETCH LIGHTLY AT FIRST!

Vulpes zerda

North Africa, Arabia.
Size: body 36 – 40 cm (14½ – 16 in);
tail 20 – 20 cm (8 – 12 in)

Fennec foxes live in groups of up to ten, and feed at night on small animals and insects. Small and agile, they live in burrows. In soft sand, they dig so quickly it can look like they're just sinking into the ground!

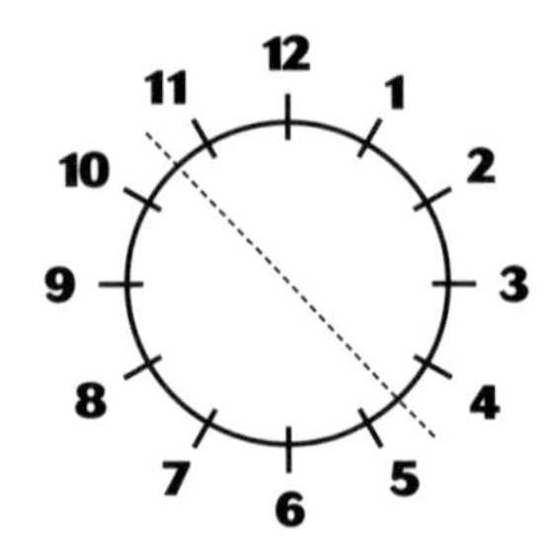

Compare the tilt of ovals and other angles with the clock face.

1. Begin by sketching the body of the fox—two tall ovals connected with curving lines.

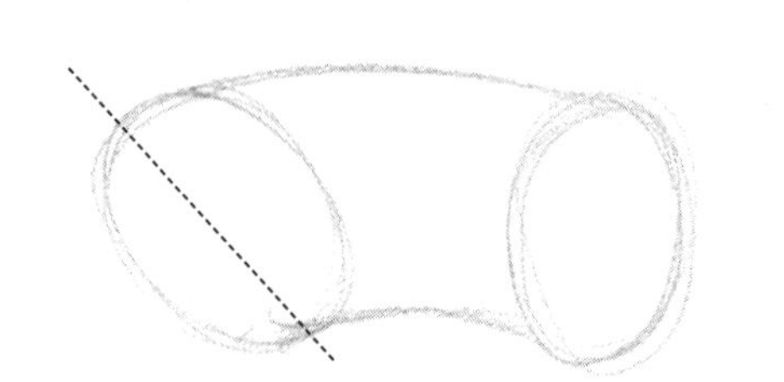

2. Sketch a light circle for the head, noting where it lies in relationship to the shoulder (arrow). Add the nose and mouth. Notice that the neck lines curve outward on both top and bottom. Draw lines for the neck.

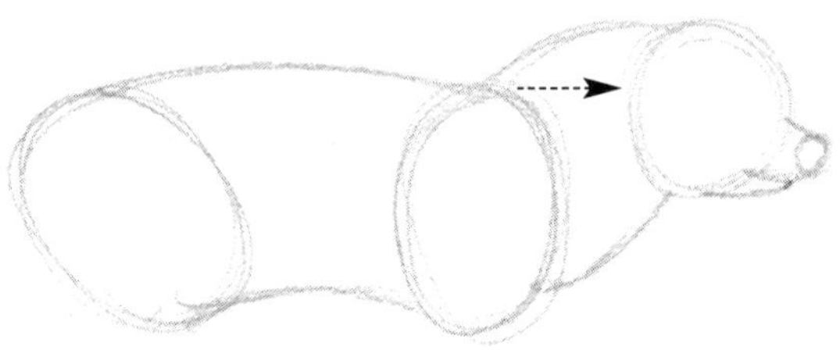

3. Darken the nose and mouth. Add the eye, with a small circle that will remain white. Draw the distinctive large ears.

4. Draw squiggly lines to form the bushy tail.

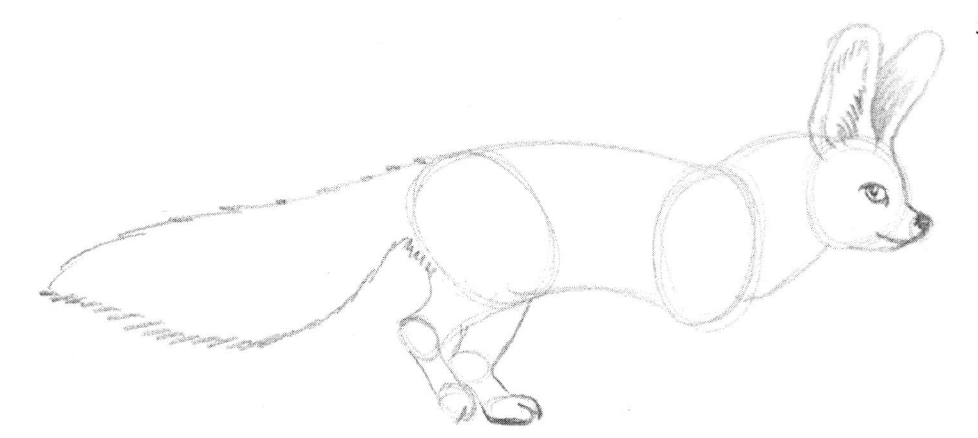

5 Sketch small circles for the leg joints. Draw the rear legs and feet. Add emphasis to the farther one, which is supporting the fox's entire weight.

6. Likewise, draw the front legs and feet. Notice that neither is completely on the ground.

7. Look at the variations in the tones (light and dark). Use short pencil strokes to create the fur of the fennec fox. Leave some areas light. Go over the outline, adding emphasis at points you think need it.

Add a slight *cast shadow* underneath the fox. Draw whiskers! Clean up any smudges with your eraser.

Fine fox! Put today's date on your drawing and save it!

Gila Monster

Heloderma suspectum

Southwest United States.
Size: 60 cm (23 in)

The slow-moving Gila (pronounced "heela") moves about mainly at night, looking for birds' eggs, small reptiles and small rodents to eat. The large tail is used to store fat, since food in the desert is not always abundant *(what other desert animals store fat?)*. Gila monsters and their relatives, Mexican Beaded Lizards, are the only venomous lizards. They take shelter under rocks or in burrows. The females lay eggs once a year, in a hole, in autumn or winter. The eggs hatch about 30 days later.

1. Sketch three flat ovals to begin your Gila drawing.

2. Add two legs with claws. Draw the small visible section of the other front leg (behind the head). Refine the shape of the head, and join the ovals together with smooth curved lines.

3. When all the parts of your Gila are in place, erase unnecessary guide lines. (A kneadable eraser works best; you can dab and twist with it, forming a point to get into tight areas.) Draw the forked tongue, eye, and mouth. Add the short pencil lines on the feet.

4. Look at the patterns on the Gila's tail—bands of light and dark, with dark or light squarish spots in them. Draw the patterns. Add scales in the light areas.

5. The body has a less regular pattern. Have fun drawing it! Add a shadow beneath the Gila, and draw some rocks and twigs near it.

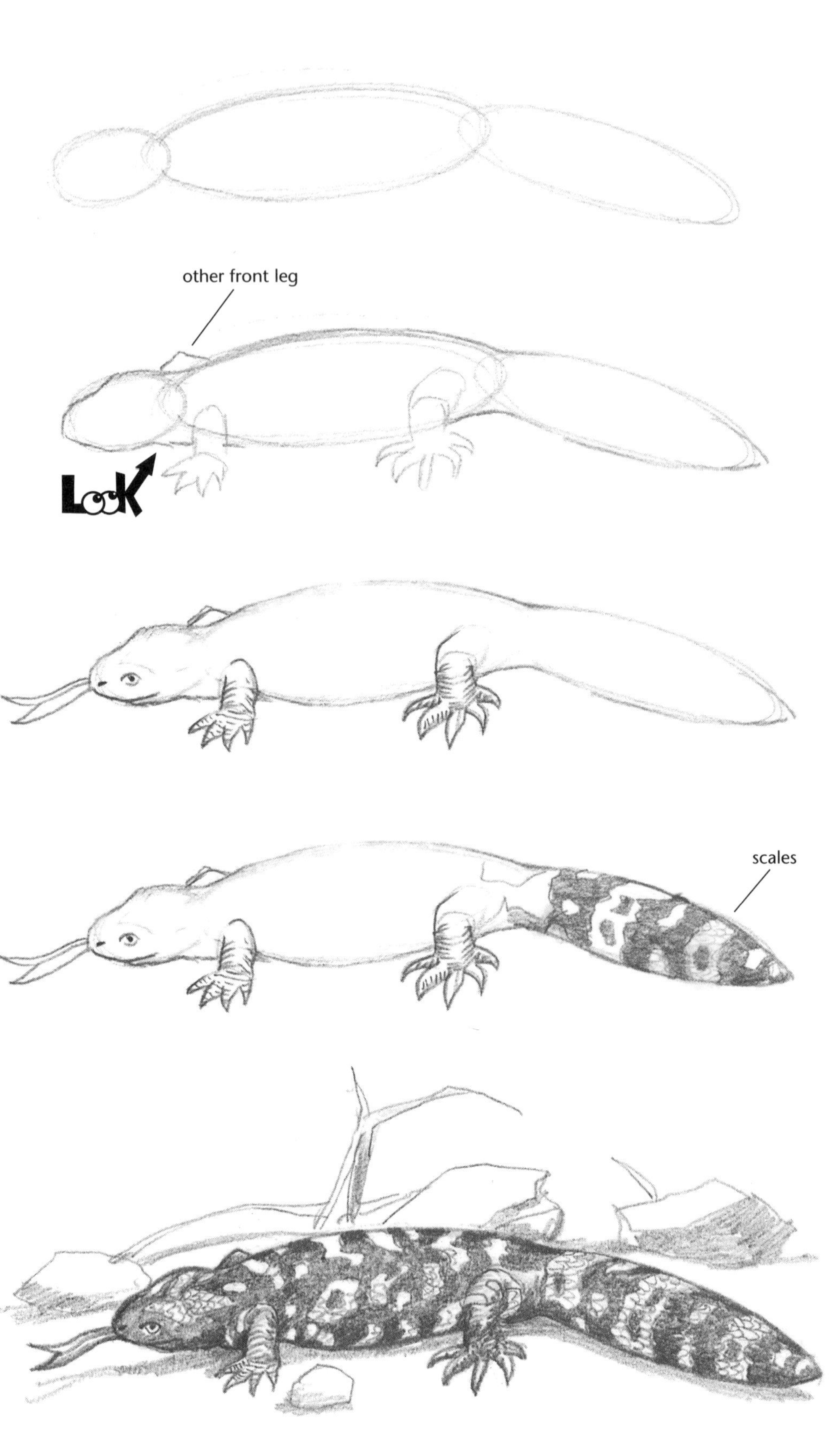

Put today's date on your drawing and save it!

Horned Toad

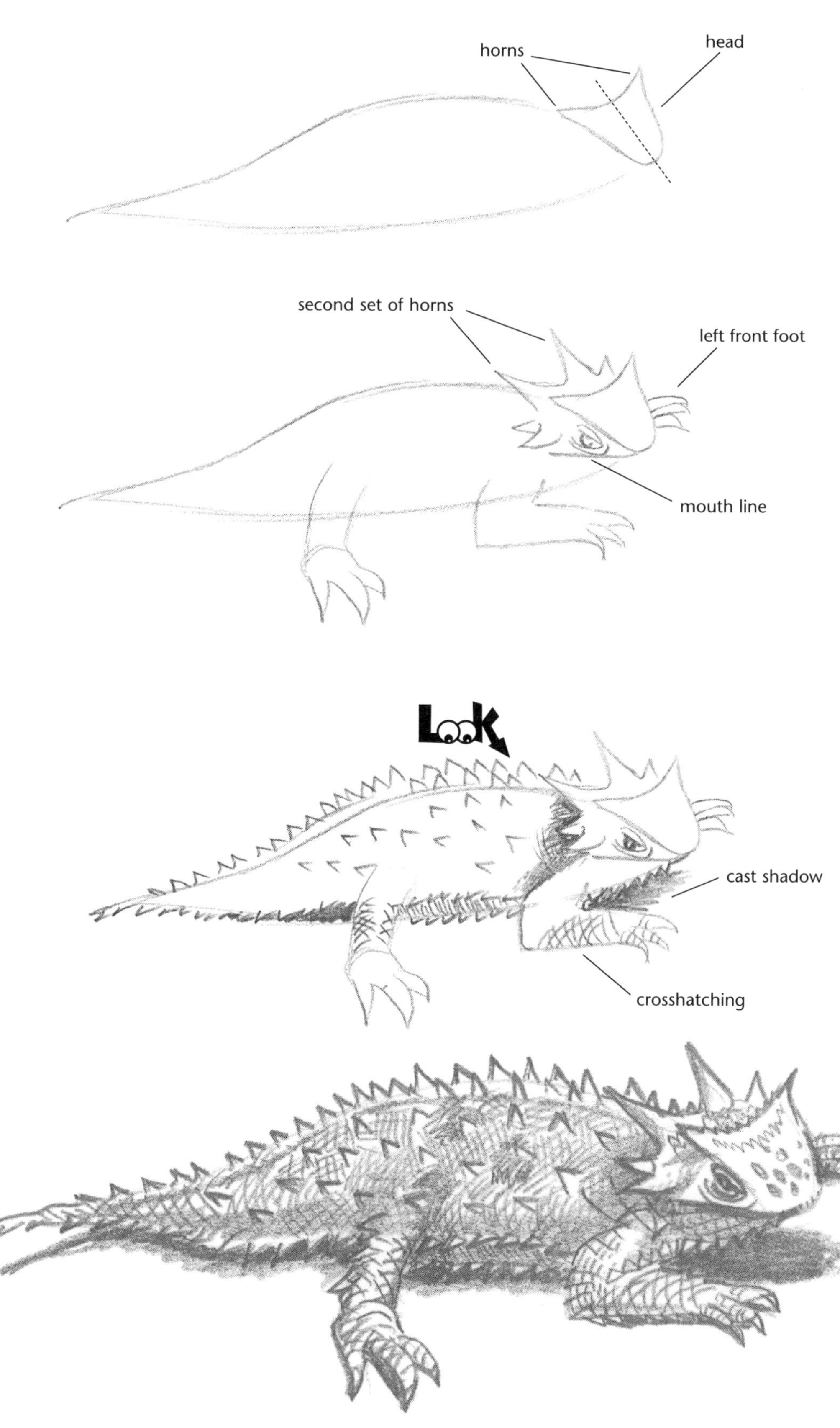

Phrynosoma douglasii

North America.
Size: 4 — 13 cm (1.6 — 5.2 in)

"That's not a toad!" you say. You're right. The name horned toad is given to a lizard, with horns or spikes on the back of the head (the only other horned lizard is the Thorny Devil of Australia). At night, it wriggles below the sand, during the day it moves about slowly and feeds on insects and ants. Horned toads (also called Texas horned lizards) lie very flat and motionless when disturbed, but can also inflate themselves, jump forward and hiss. And–who knows how–they can even squirt blood from their eyes!

1. Lightly sketch curved lines for the top and bottom of the body. Add the tilted shape that makes the top of the head—rounded at the front and pointed at the back for the horns.

2. Add the second set of horns. Draw the eye and the mouth line. Lightly sketch the two visible legs, with claws. Draw the claws of the left front foot.

3. *Now look at the details!* Add a row of spikes along the back and scattered on the body. Add a *cast shadow* for contrast under the chin and behind the horns. Use *crosshatching* to create scales.

   Following this example, add more shading, shadows, and *crosshatching*. Leave the head lighter than the body. This makes the head, eye, and spikes, the focal point of the drawing.

   Put today's date on your drawing and save it!

Jerboa

ALWAYS SKETCH LIGHTLY AT FIRST!

Dipus sagitta (northern three-toed)

North Africa, Asia.
Size: body 10-13 cm (4 – 5¼ in);
tail 15 – 19 cm (6 – 7½ in)

Like the kangaroo rat of the United States, jerboas live in a burrow, coming out only at night when the surface temperature has cooled off from the heat of the day. In autumn, they dig a deeper burrow to hibernate. In the spring, they may have two litters, with 2-5 young each. A jerboa gets all the water it needs from its food, which includes seeds, roots, and insect larvae.

1. Lightly sketch a horizontal, slightly tilted oval for the jerboa's body. Sketch the oval of the leg overlapping the oval of the body. Add another, smaller, almost round oval for the head.

2. From the leg oval, draw the first section of leg, with a small circle for the ankle joint. From there, draw the next section and the foot. Sketch a small circle for the elbow, and draw the front paw.

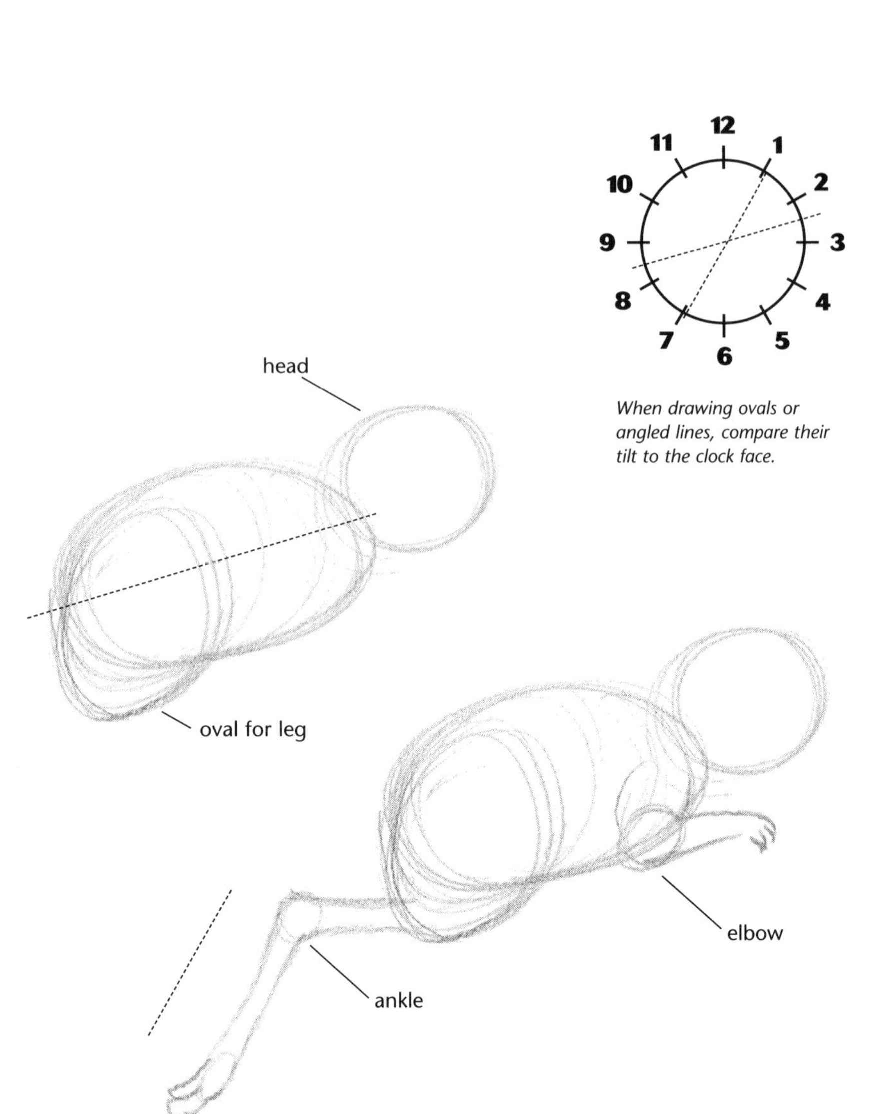

When drawing ovals or angled lines, compare their tilt to the clock face.

Climate control
By digging beneath the scorching hot surface of the desert, jerboas and their relatives, kangaroo rats, manage to stay cool during the day. At night, when the surface cools, they emerge to search for food.

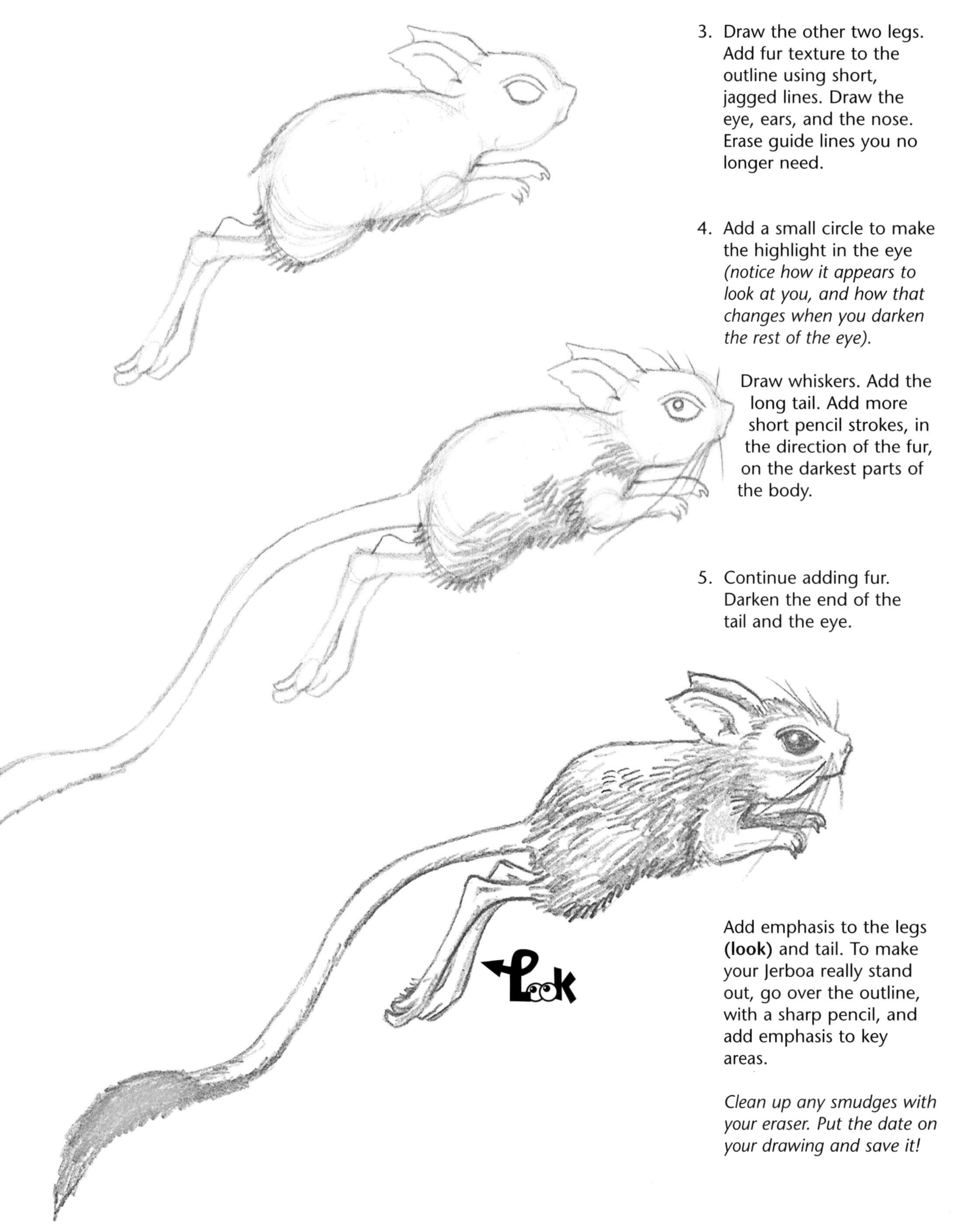

3. Draw the other two legs. Add fur texture to the outline using short, jagged lines. Draw the eye, ears, and the nose. Erase guide lines you no longer need.

4. Add a small circle to make the highlight in the eye *(notice how it appears to look at you, and how that changes when you darken the rest of the eye).*

Draw whiskers. Add the long tail. Add more short pencil strokes, in the direction of the fur, on the darkest parts of the body.

5. Continue adding fur. Darken the end of the tail and the eye.

Add emphasis to the legs **(look)** and tail. To make your Jerboa really stand out, go over the outline, with a sharp pencil, and add emphasis to key areas.

Clean up any smudges with your eraser. Put the date on your drawing and save it!

Lanner Falcon

Falco biarmicus

North Africa, Middle East.
Size: Body 40 – 45 cm (16 – 18 in); wingspan 70 – 80 cm (25 – 27 in)

Falco means sickle, and refers to the curved claws of falcons. Falcons swoop down and grab birds out of the air. People have trained them for thousands of years, to catch food and also as a sport. Falcons don't build nests; they either take over an abandoned nest from another bird, or lay their eggs on high ledges.

1. *Lightly* sketch the tall, slightly tilted oval of the falcon's body. Above it, add a small oval for the head. Leaving space for the shoulder **(look)**, add the curving lines.

2. Draw the curving beak, with the characteristic double notch of a falcon. Draw a line back for the mouth. In the center of the head, draw the curve of the eyebrow, and then the round eye under it.

3. Sketch the two legs, each with a thick feathered portion. Sketch the feet with claws. Add a jagged line to make the top of a rock for the falcon to perch on.

4. Study the falcon's shoulders and wings before drawing them. Add the shoulder beneath the falcon's beak, then the outside and inside of the wing beneath it. Draw the curve of the wing on the other side—see how it extends behind, to the other side of the body. Draw lines for the tail feathers.

5. Erase guide lines you no longer need.

   Very carefully, with a sharp pencil, shade the head with short strokes radiating from the mouth and beak.

   Shade the tail feathers. Go over the outlines of the wings, legs and feet with a sharp pencil. Add jagged lines where feathers stick out slightly at the edge of the leg.

6. Notice the details and shading in this drawing. With a sharp pencil, add details: the marks on the breast feathers, claws, or details on the rock. As your pencil becomes duller, add the softer shading.

   Every once in a while, sit back from your drawing and take stock—really look at it and appreciate your progress. Do you see any other details you need to add? Add them.

Falco fabuloso! Clean up any smudges, date and save your drawing!

Pallas's Cat

ALWAYS SKETCH LIGHTLY AT FIRST!

Felis manul

Central Asia.
Size: 71 – 86 cm (28 – 38 in)

This elusive cat lives in caves, rock crevices, or burrows taken from other animals such as marmots. It only comes to hunt at night, preying on mice, birds, and small hares. The fur color varies from pale gray to yellowish to reddish-brown. Pallas's cat has the longest, densest fur of any wild cat.

Here's a good example of using form to add realism to a drawing. The shape of the cat's body may look like a sack of potatoes, but there are bones and muscles underneath the skin. Understanding a little about them is the key to having your drawing not look like "Pallas's Potato Sack."

1. Sketch three light, overlapping circles. You don't need to sketch the hidden part of each circle.

2. The body is fairly easy, but the face may be tricky, so complete it first. Near the center of the head circle, draw a small triangular nose; above it, to either side, draw the expressive eyes.

3. Draw the distinctive dark markings on the cheeks. Add the mouth, with a shadow underneath. Draw a line connecting the mouth to the nose.

4. From the nose, go up and out, straight past each eye, and draw the short ears. From the nose up, use short upward pencil strokes for fur. Add spots on the forehead. Continue adding fur lines radiating outward around the face.

5. Sketch a tall, tilting oval for the top of the rear leg. Sketch a small circle for the ankle joint and add the rear leg and paw. Draw the front leg and paw. Add a little shading with short pencil strokes to remind you of the form of the leg under the fur, even though you can't really see it.

   Finish shading the face, and add whiskers.

6. Sketch the tail, with its dark rings. Carefully add the visible part of the other two legs.

7. Paying close attention to dark and light areas, go over the entire cat with short pencil strokes in the direction of the fur. Add the stripe marks on the back and side, showing the round *contour.* Draw a *cast shadow* underneath. **Look** at the way lines create texture in the *cast shadow.*

Purrfect! Clean up any smudges with your eraser. Date and save your drawing in your portfolio!

Roadrunner

Geococcyx californianus

North America.
Size: 58 cm (23 in) including tail

The roadrunner is a species of cuckoo. It makes quick dashes, then stops suddenly and looks around. If it sees food–a lizard, small snake, grasshopper or insect–it dashes after it, making quick turns if necessary. Roadrunners make neat nests in trees or cactus clumps, lining them with leaves, feathers, even snake skins and bones!

1. Look carefully at the angle of each oval, and compare its tilt to the clock face. Lightly sketch the two ovals. Connect them with curved lines to make the roadrunner's neck.

2. Draw the long and slightly curved beak. Add the eye. Notice the direction the scraggly neck feathers point. Draw them. Add the dark patch behind the eye.

3. See the limp lizard hanging from the roadrunner's beak? Notice how the legs of the lizard hang and point downward. Also notice that part of this lizard's tail is missing...!

   Draw the lizard and *then* draw the lower part of the beak.

4. Draw a line showing the edge of the wing. Add feathers. On the bird's belly, add short lines to make it look fluffy, in contrast to the neck feathers. Look carefully at the angles of the leg and foot. From the back of the body, draw one leg and foot, with three of its four claws visible.

5. Add the second leg, at a different angle than the first leg. Draw the branch on which the roadrunner sits. Draw long pencil strokes to begin the tail.

6. Draw the tail roughly the length of the body. Outline and darken the wing and tail feathers. Add shading and contour lines to the legs and feet. Use varied pencil lines to add texture to the branch.

OK, roadrunner– thanks for posing. You can eat your supper now!

Put today's date on your drawing and save it!

Sandgrouse

ALWAYS SKETCH LIGHTLY AT FIRST!

Syrrhaptes paradoxus

Central Asia, southern Siberia, southern Mongolia – northern China. Size: 25 – 48 cm (10 – 19 in)

Sandgrouses are related to doves and pigeons. The desert dwellers eat only very dry seeds, so they need to drink every day. After drinking their fill at a watering spot, they then soak their bellies in water and fly back (as far as 30 km (19 miles!) to their young, which drink the water from the belly feathers. Pallas's sandgrouse performs "eruptions" every once in a while: suddenly large numbers leave their home and fly tens of thousands of kilometers east or west. No one knows why.

Leave room for the tail!

throat

1. Look at the finished drawing. As you start your drawing, remember to leave room for the tail! Sketch two light ovals, for the body and head.

2. Add the beak, eye, and facial markings. Draw short, curving pencil strokes for the feathers of the throat.

3. Add swooping lines for the upward curving wing and tail. Look carefully at the feet, and draw them.

4. The last step involves observation, patience, and time. Carefully observe the location, direction, and shading of the various wing and tail feathers. Do "soft" shading when your pencil gets dull; use your freshly sharpened point to go over outlines.

   Clean up any smudges with your eraser, put today's date on your drawing and save it in your portfolio!

Scarab Beetle

family Scarabaeidae, Africa.

Scarab beetles, also known as dung beetles, roll dung into balls larger than themselves. The female lays eggs in it, and it provides nourishment for the larva after they hatch. The ancient Egyptians considered scarab beetles sacred, since the dung balls reminded them of the sun.

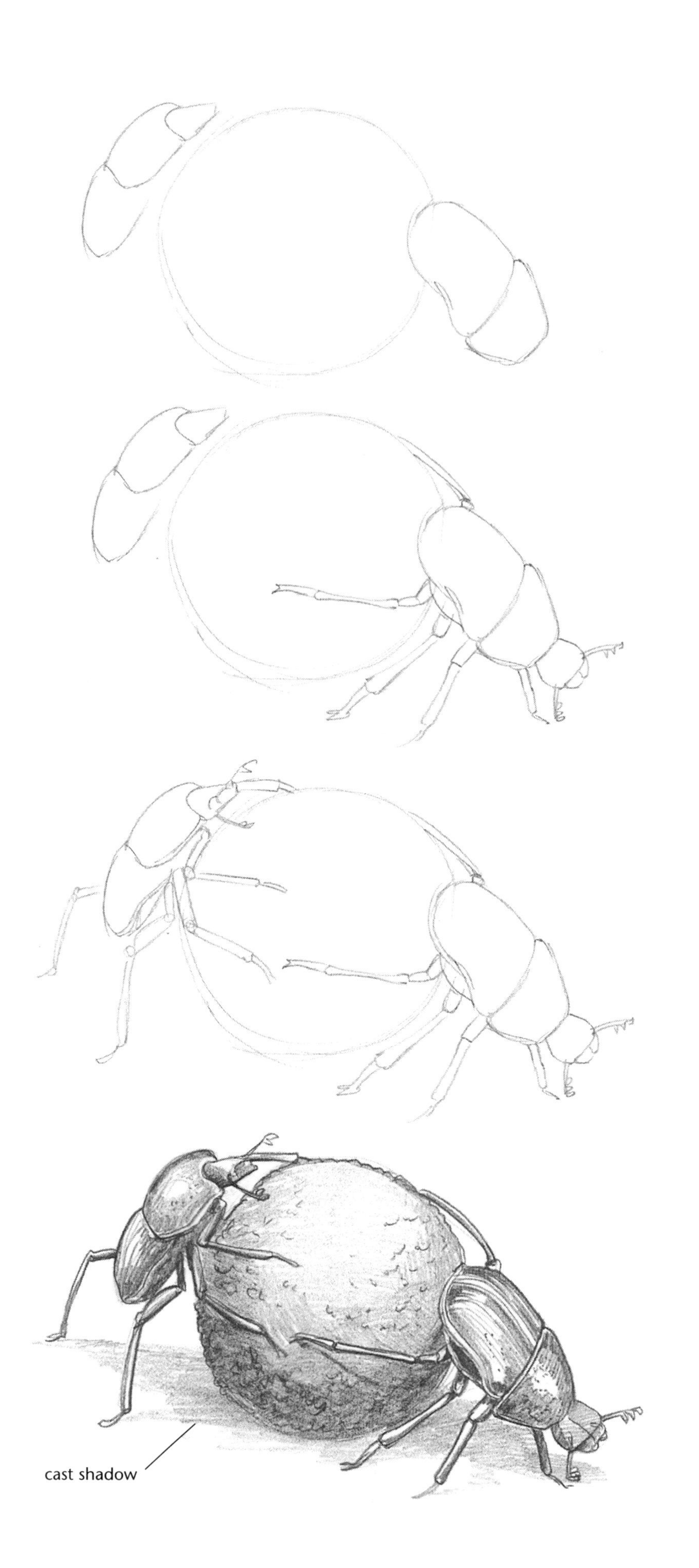

1. Possibly the most difficult part of this drawing is getting the dung ball round! Start by lightly sketching the circle for the dung ball, and see if you can get it as round as the beetles do! Next, add the main body parts of each beetle.

2. Look at the front beetle. See the angle of each section of each leg. Add the segmented legs, a head and antennae to the front beetle.

3. See the rear beetle. As with the front beetle, pay close attention to the angle of each section of each leg. Add its legs, head and antennae.

4. Notice how the beetles shine, while the dung ball looks dull. As you add shading and details, pay close attention to light and dark. Add a *cast shadow* beneath.

   Clean up any smudges with your eraser, put today's date on your drawing. and save it in your portfolio.

   You dung good!

Scorpion

ALWAYS SKETCH LIGHTLY AT FIRST!

order *Scorpiones*
Size: body 3 mm – 8 cm (⅛ in – 3 in)

About 600 different species of scorpion are known. They have one main part of their body, then five segments forming the "tail," at the end of which is the poisonous stinger. Scorpions live in cracks, but can dig their own resting places as well. At night, they eat beetles, cockroaches, and other arthropods. With their pincers (pedipalps) they bring prey to their chelicerae (jaws), which they use to tear it apart. They only sting when they need to subdue large or struggling prey. American and North African desert scorpions have the worst sting – one Sahara scorpion's sting can kill a dog in a few seconds.

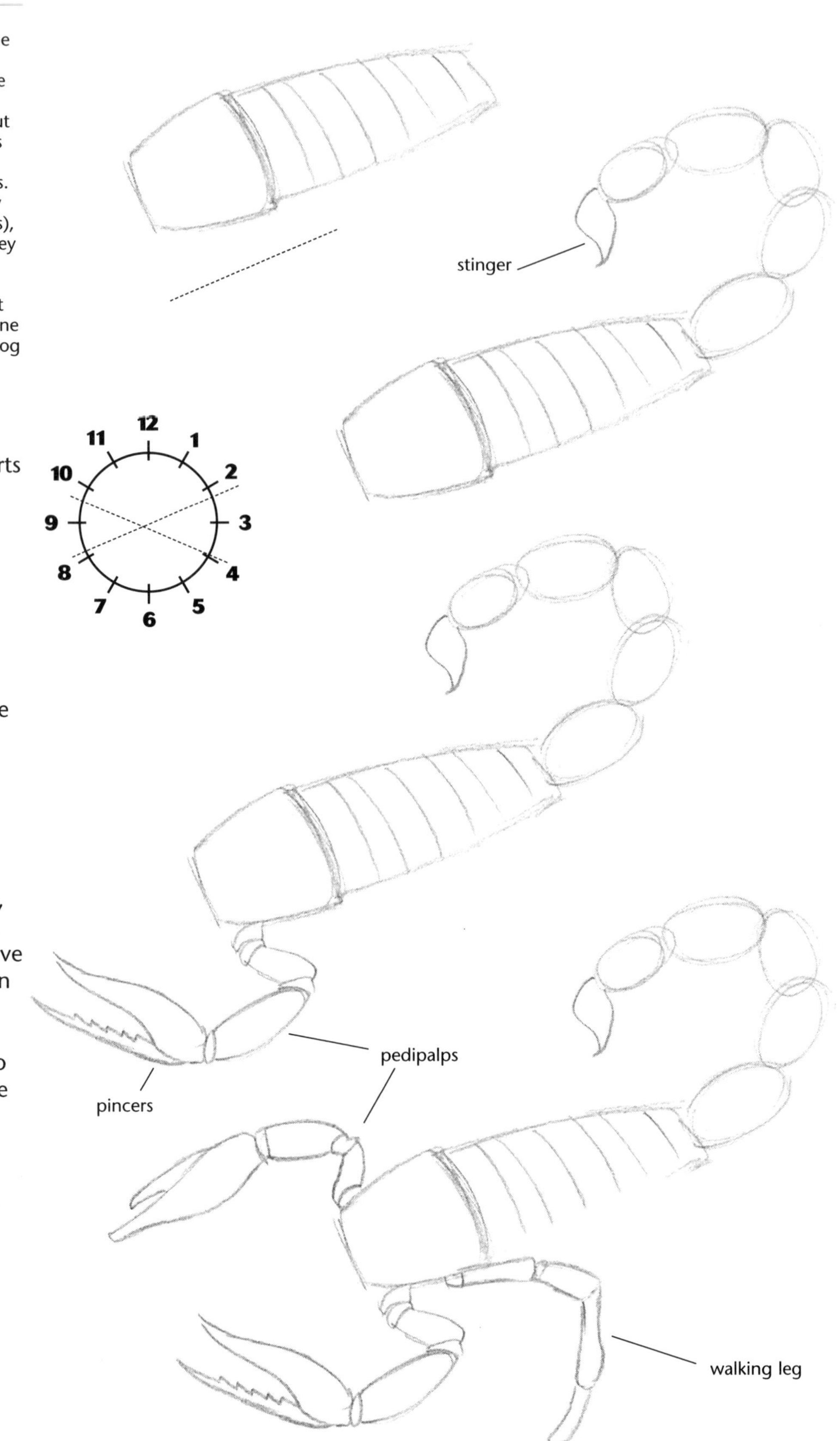

1. Sketch the two main parts of the body at an angle (compare with clock face).

2. Sketch five connected ovals for the tail, and the stinger at the end.

3. Notice the three main sections of the pedipalp, with smaller connecting sections. Carefully observe the angle of each section *before drawing.*

   Draw the first of the two pedipalps, with the large pincers at its end.

4. Add the other pedipalp, and the first of the walking legs.

5. Do you see how the remaining three walking legs *overlap* **(look)** one another? While more difficult to draw, this helps make your drawing look more real, because *overlapping* adds *depth.*

   Draw the remaining three walking legs on the scorpion's left side.

6. On the far side, fewer segments of each leg are visible. Look carefully, and draw them.

   Compare angles to the clock face to keep your lines running in the right direction.

   Add lines on the tail sections.

7. What's different in the final drawing? Add shading *(but note which parts are left light)*. Add a *cast shadow* underneath. Put a few hairs on the tail, and—what has the scorpion caught? Draw part of the pedipalp of another scorpion, which has just lost a fight to yours.

   Put today's date on your drawing and save it!

Sidewinder

Crotalus cerastes

Southwest United States.
Size: 60 – 70 cm (24 – 28 in)

The sidewinder rattlesnake moves uniquely through the desert sand: only two parts of its body touch the ground at once! Sidewinding leaves a series of J-shaped marks in the sand. Usually sidewinders hunt at night for small lizards and rodents, and rest during the day–under a bush or in another animal's burrow.

1. Start your drawing with two curving lines. Make the top line connect to the middle of the bottom line.

2. Add a second curved line below each of the first two. Draw the outline of the sidewinder's head.

3. Add upward-curving lines to connect the ends of the first lines you drew. Make sure the lower curve aligns with the other curving side.

4. Add two more small upward-curving lines to complete the other side of the snake's body. Add the end of the tail, with rattles on the tip.

5. Look carefully at the curves representing the bottom of the snake. Add contour lines to the snake's underside.

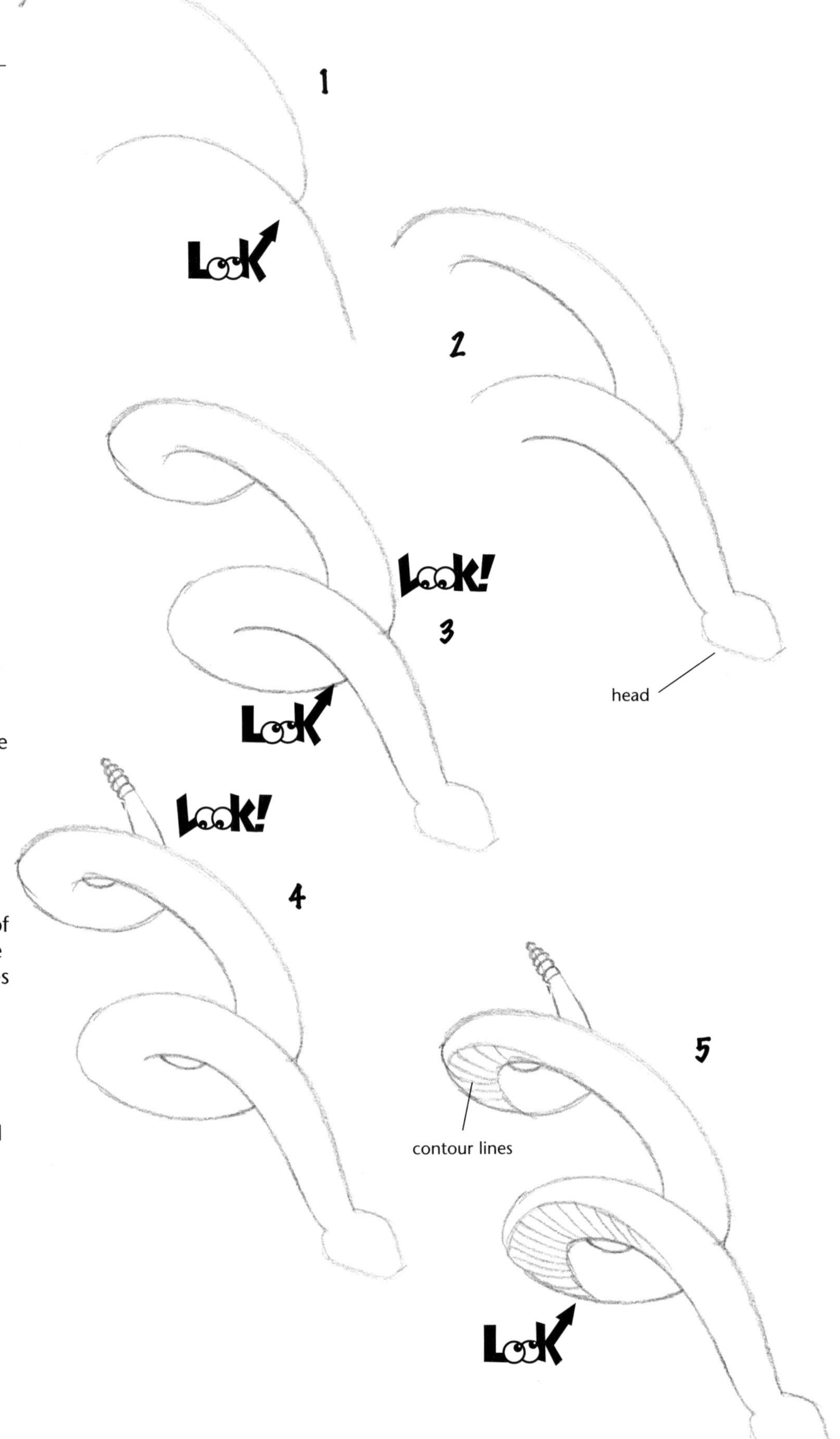

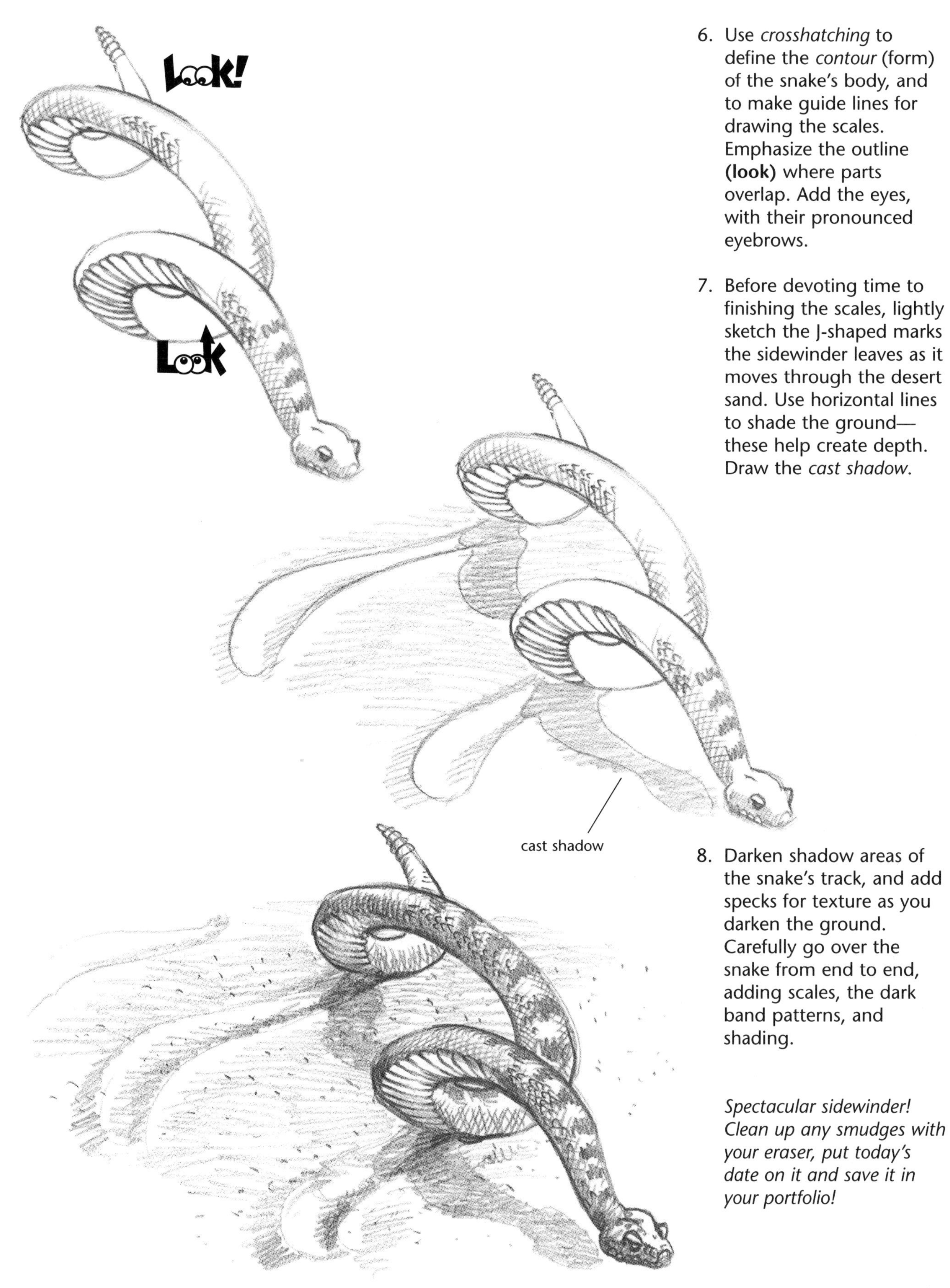

6. Use *crosshatching* to define the *contour* (form) of the snake's body, and to make guide lines for drawing the scales. Emphasize the outline **(look)** where parts overlap. Add the eyes, with their pronounced eyebrows.

7. Before devoting time to finishing the scales, lightly sketch the J-shaped marks the sidewinder leaves as it moves through the desert sand. Use horizontal lines to shade the ground—these help create depth. Draw the *cast shadow*.

8. Darken shadow areas of the snake's track, and add specks for texture as you darken the ground. Carefully go over the snake from end to end, adding scales, the dark band patterns, and shading.

Spectacular sidewinder! Clean up any smudges with your eraser, put today's date on it and save it in your portfolio!

Spotted Skunk

Spilogale gracilis

North America.
Size: 33 – 56 cm (13 – 22 in)

Spotted skunks usually den underground, but also climb trees. No two skunks have exactly the same color pattern. They eat rodents, birds, eggs, insects, and fruit. In the southern part of their range (central Mexico) they give birth any time of the year. Farther north, they give birth in the spring to 4-5 young, after a gestation of 4 months. Before spraying its unpleasant smelly spray, a spotted skunk warns its enemies by doing a handstand.

ALWAYS SKETCH LIGHTLY AT FIRST!

1. Before you draw, note that the shoulder oval lies slightly lower than the head oval. Lightly sketch the two small ovals. Leave room above for the rest of the body! Connect the two ovals with a curved line for the neck. Sketch a small circle for the nose, and draw lines to connect it to the head.

2. From the shoulder oval, draw two lines at a slight angle for the leg. Add an oval for the foot. Draw claws. Draw the other leg and foot. Draw the eye, nose and mouth.

3. Far above the head and leg, sketch a larger, tilted oval. Draw two curved lines to connect the back leg oval with the head and shoulder ovals.

4. Sketch ovals for the rear leg joints. Add the leg and claws. With curving pencil strokes, draw the hairs of the tail, pointing up, then falling back down. Add the ear, whiskers, and short pencil strokes on the front leg for hair.

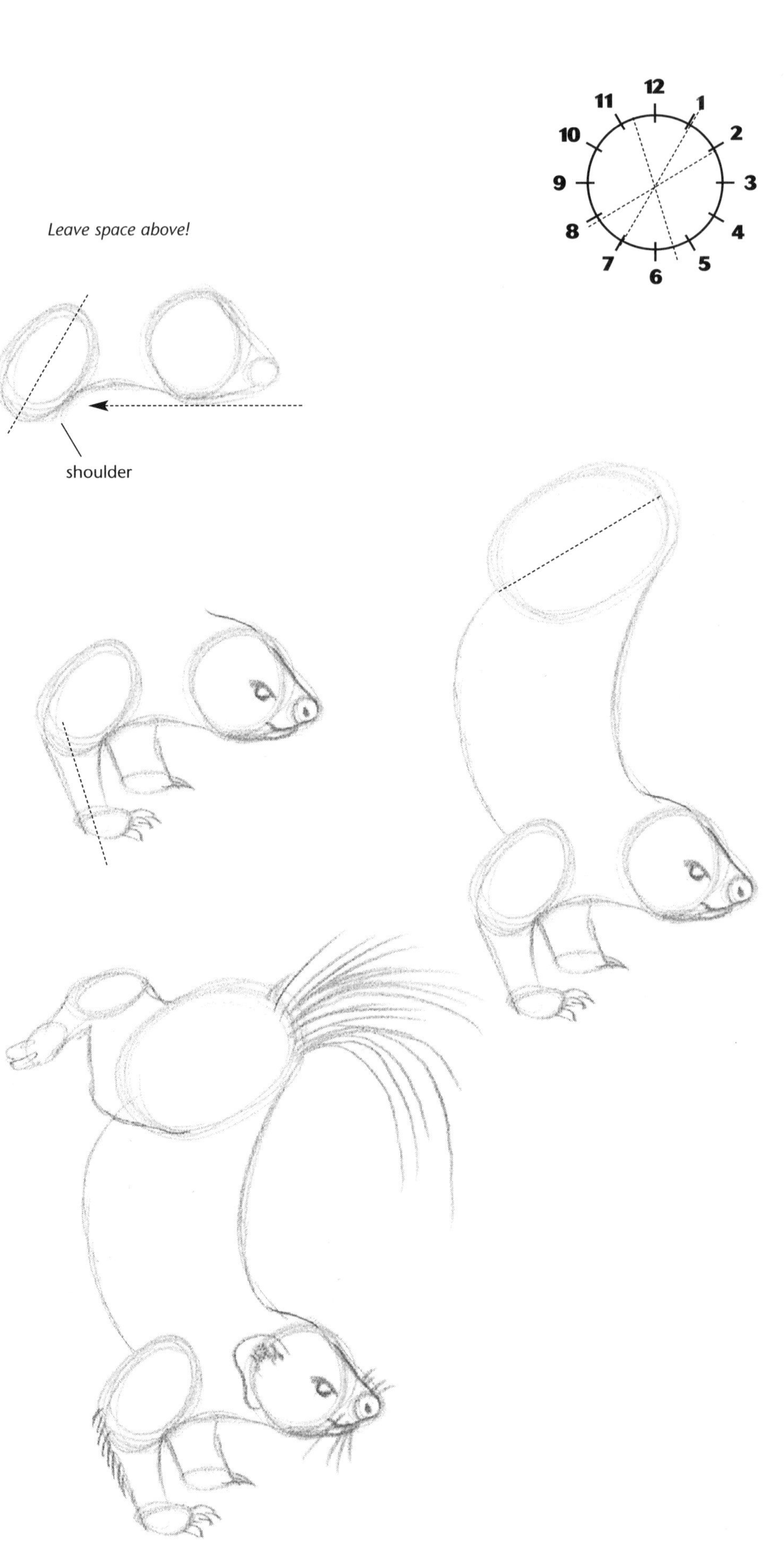

5. With a sharp pencil, go over the outline, using short back and forth movements–almost like scribbles–to add texture to places where fur sticks out. Lightly "map out" the white spots and stripes for your skunk–remember, each is unique!

6. Look! Notice how the dark areas don't appear completely black. Using short back and forth pencil strokes, always in the direction of the fur, make the whole skunk, except for the white spots, dark. Leave highlight areas slightly lighter; make shadow areas slightly darker. When the tones are correct, add a few more crisp pencil strokes to emphasize the texture of the fur.

Question:
What do you say to a spotted skunk doing a handstand?

Answer:
"Goodbye."

OK, another:
How do you say "goodbye" to a skunk doing a handstand?

Answer:
As fast as you can!

Did you pick up some smudges on your drawing? It's easy to do, and also easy to avoid. Get in the habit of putting a piece of clean paper under your hand to protect parts you've already drawn.

Put today's date on your drawing and save it in your portfolio!

Tarantula

North America.
Size: body up to 7.5 cm (3 in) long;
leg span to 30 cm (12 in)

The tarantula is a kind of wolf spider *(Lycosa)*. When threatened, a tarantula might rear up on its hind legs and make a hissing noise. Unlike other spiders, the jaws of the tarantula move up and down instead of sideways. While it is a big, scary looking spider, the tarantula's bite is not as bad as people sometimes think: it's similar to a wasp sting.

1. Lightly sketch a horizontal oval for the spider's abdomen, and a rounder one for the cephalothorax. Add the eight eyes, and the visible part of the jaws (the fangs point down, so you don't see them from this angle).

2. Draw the two most extended legs first, starting with the coxa and trochanter, thence proceeding to depict the femur, patella, tibia, metatarsus, and tarsus. (!)

3. The other two legs are *foreshortened* (coming toward you in the picture), so you don't see the full complement of parts *(I'll bet that's OK with you!)*.

   Draw them as you see them, using the clock face as a guide for angles.

4. Add a little more definition to the cephalothorax by making slight rounded indents where each leg attaches. Draw the thick pedipalps.

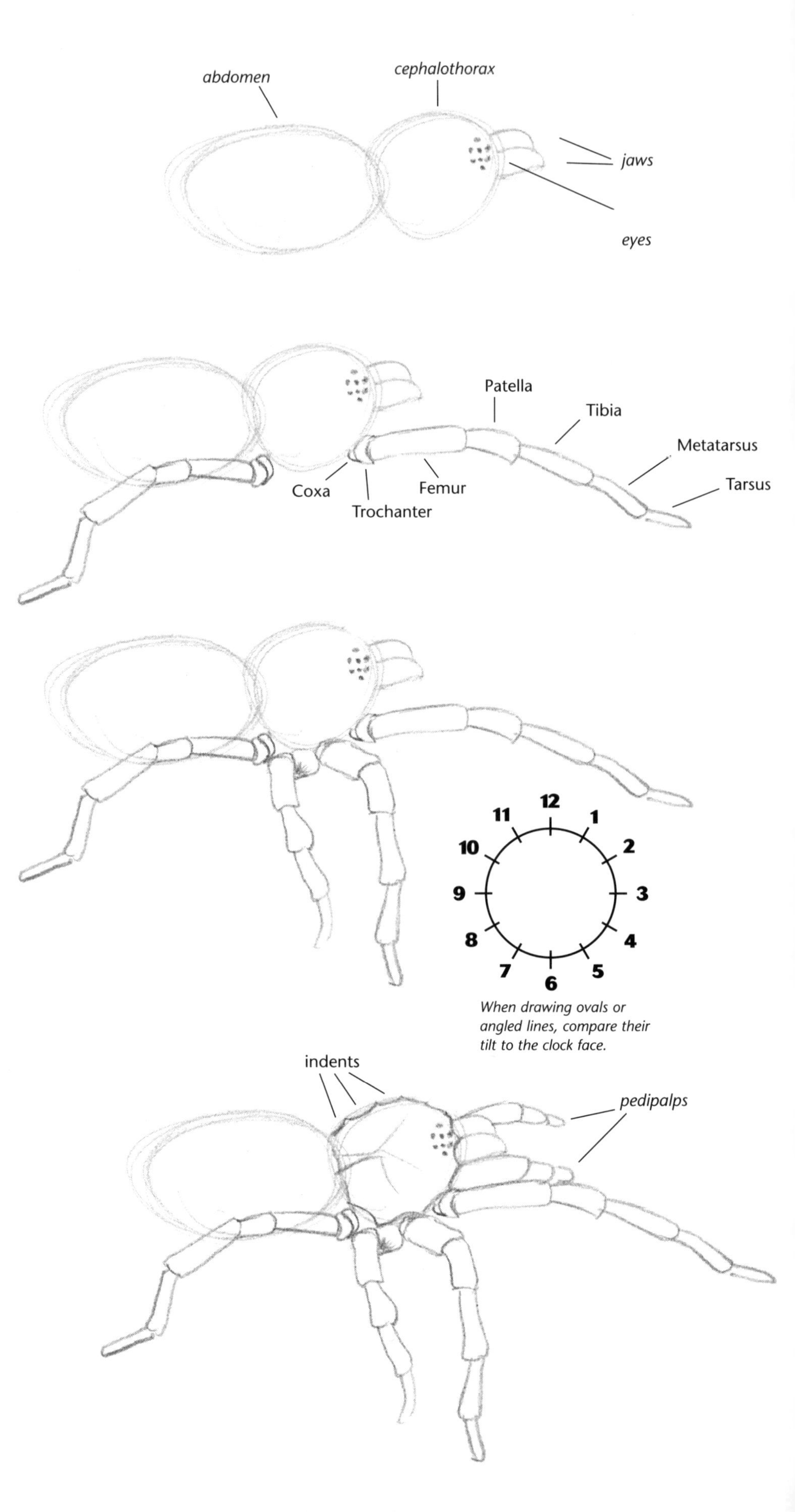

When drawing ovals or angled lines, compare their tilt to the clock face.

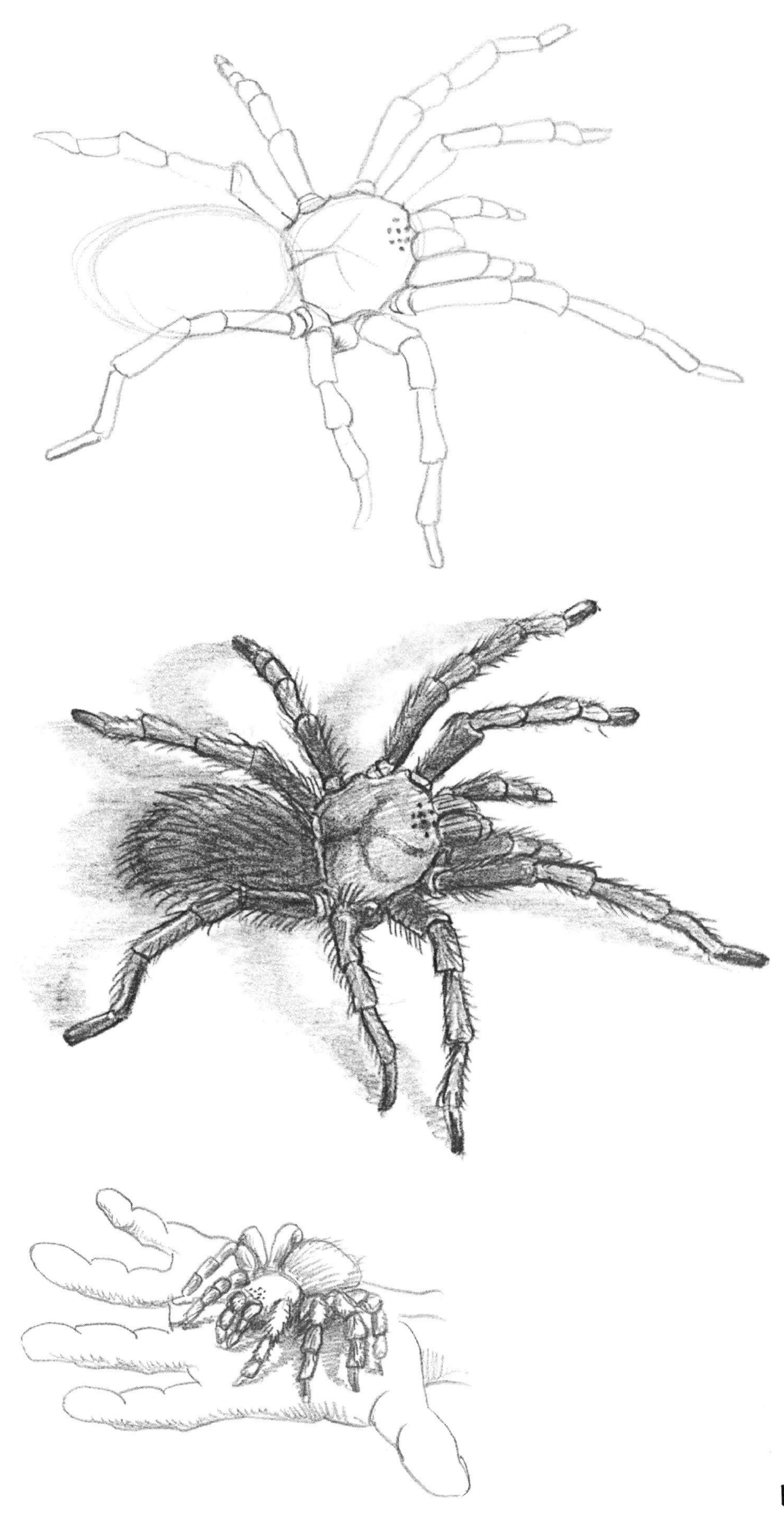

5. You'll find the legs on the other side easier to draw, since there is little *foreshortening*. Add them one segment at a time.

As you can see, the last step involves some time. Are you ready to keep going on this drawing, or do you want to keep it as a practice sketch and start another? Your choice. Put the date on this drawing and save it if you do decide to start over.

6. Finish your tarantula by shading the body parts with a dull pencil, then adding short pencil strokes for hairs when the pencil is sharp.

   With a dull pencil (and perhaps smearing it a bit with your finger or a small wad of paper), add the *cast shadow* beneath.

You can have fun adding a hand to your drawing to show scale. Don't know how to draw a hand? Maybe you want to practice on a separate sheet, and draw it before you draw the spider!

Tantalizing tarantula! Clean up any smudges with your eraser, put today's date on it and save it in your portfolio!

Thorny devil

Moloch horridus

Australia. Size: 15 cm (6 in)

This small desert lizard (also known as the *Australian moloch)* looks larger because of the points all over its body. The points keep predators away (would *you* eat something that thorny?). It moves slowly, and likes to eat ants–one at a time, sitting for hours by an ant nest. At night, dew drops form on the lizard's skin: this is how the Thorny Devil gets water to drink!

1. Sketch a long, slightly tilted oval for the body. Sketch a smaller oval for the head, tilting the opposite way. Connect them with lines for the neck.

2. Add lines for the legs and claws. Draw the tail.

   Add a line underneath for the ground.

3. Look at this thorny devil! At the front of the head, draw the eye and mouth. Add spikes on the chin and top of the head.

   Add a jagged edge to the bottom of the tail. Draw spikes on the front and rear leg. Make smaller spikes on each of the claws.

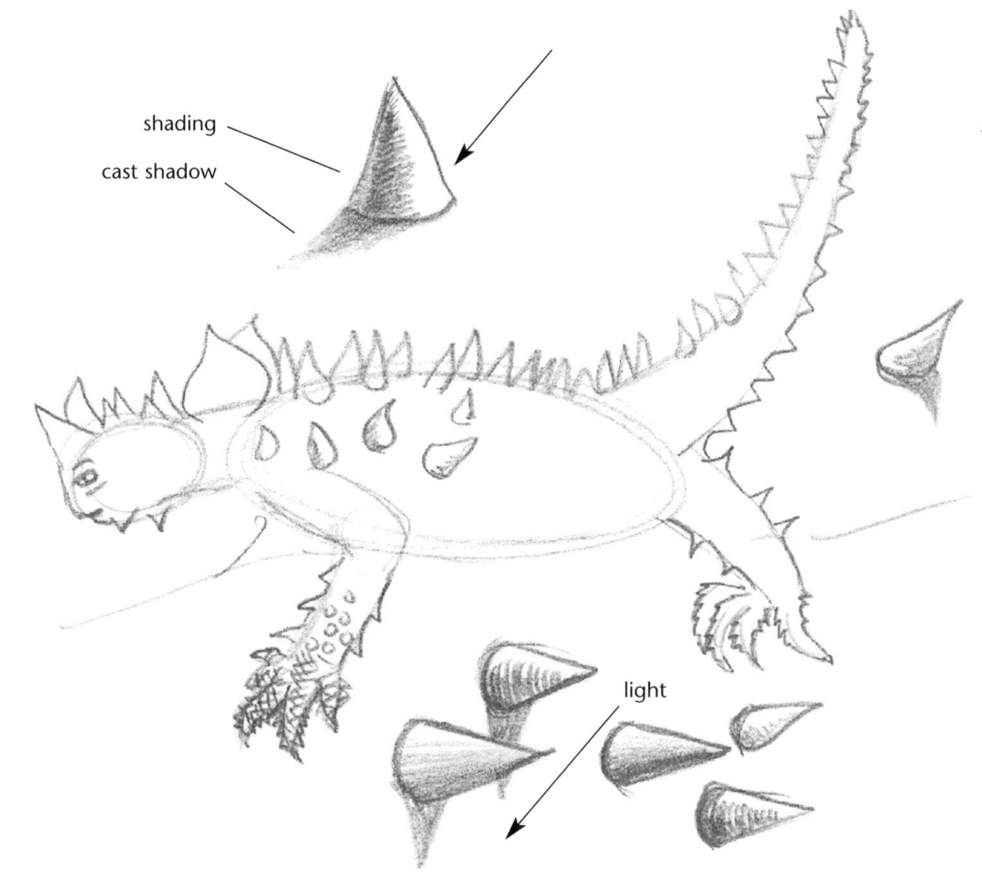

4. Before you start going wild with spikes, take a moment to study the various cones you see here. The rounded spikes on the Moloch's back are really little cones; you don't have to draw them as carefully as these examples, but you'll find it helpful to see how the shadows of the cones look.

   Draw more spikes along the lizard's back, and start adding those little cone-shaped spikes.

   On the legs, make small circles, tightly packed together, for scales.

5. Go wild with spikes! Then add shading and the darker areas of the lizard's camouflage pattern. Make a *cast shadow* beneath.

   Mahvelous Moloch! Clean up any smudges with your eraser. Put the date on your drawing and save it!

cast shadow

Trapdoor Spider

ALWAYS SKETCH LIGHTLY AT FIRST!

family Ctenizidae

Worldwide.

Trap-door spiders dig burrows, covering the opening with a hinged flap made from silk and dirt. Then they sit and wait until an unwary insect wanders close to the door, and ZIP!–they push the door open, jump on the insect, and drag it back into the tunnel to kill and eat it.

1. Start your drawing with two upside-down L shapes for the tunnel. Lightly draw the two ovals of the spider's body—the abdomen and cephalothorax.

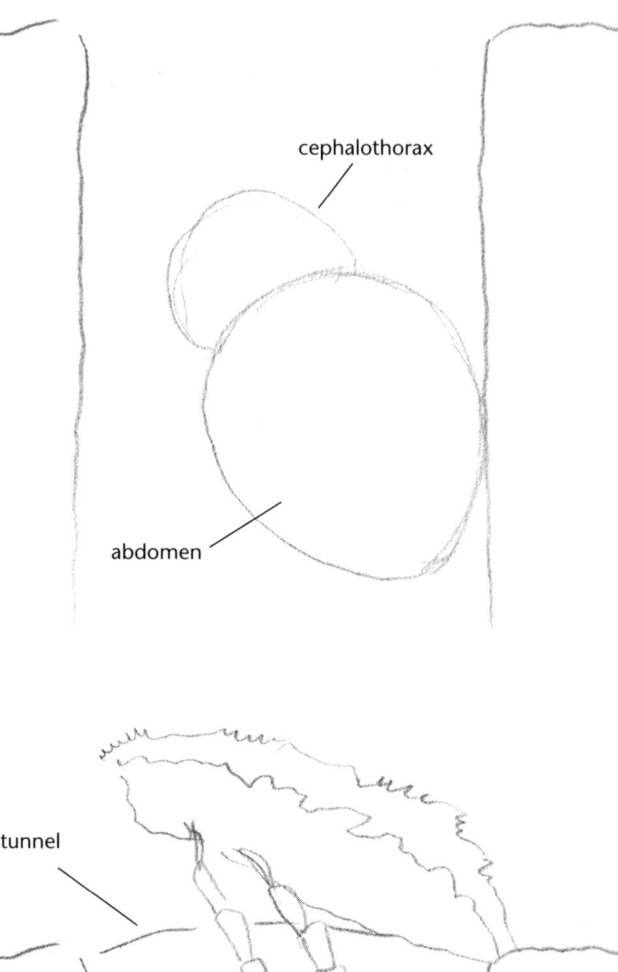

2. From the cephalothorax, draw two segmented legs reaching upward. Add the pedipalps, eight tiny eyes, and jaws (in this top view, you can't see the fangs).

   Look at the squiggly shaped trap door. Draw the trap door and a line for the edge of the tunnel.

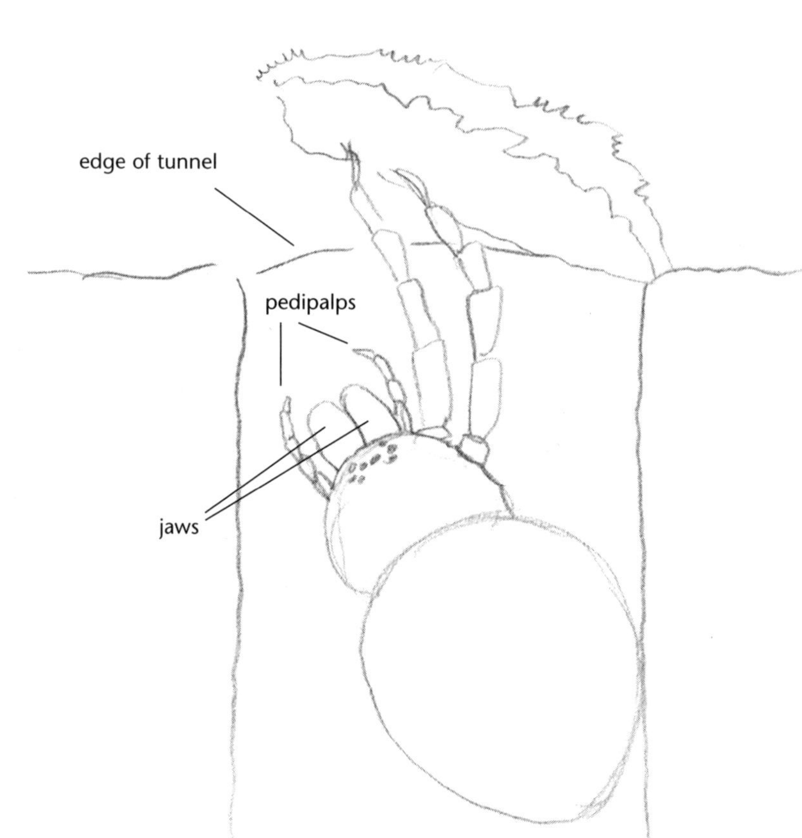

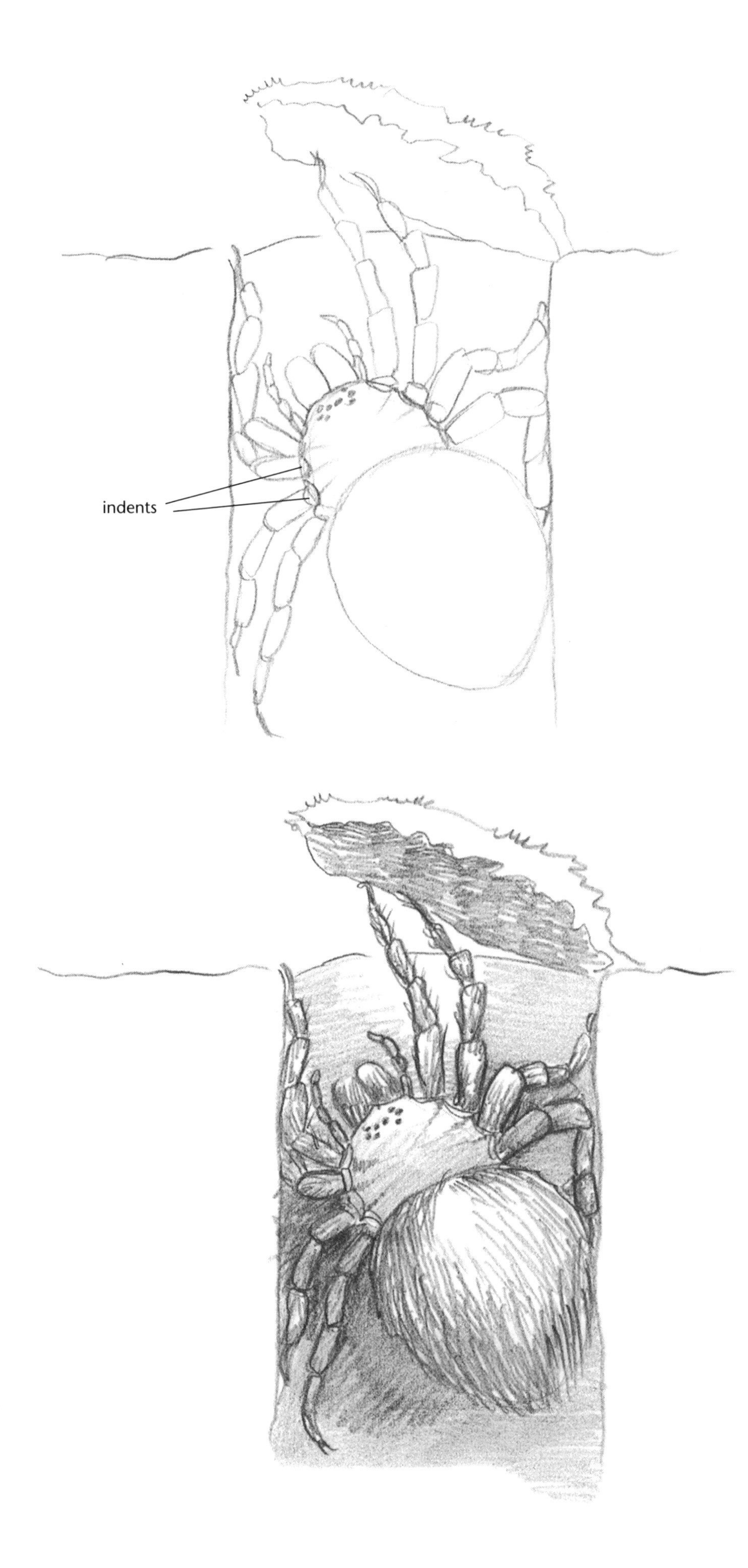

3. Add the remaining legs, one at a time. Draw indents on the cephalothorax at the point where each leg attaches.

4. With a sharp pencil, make short strokes to shade the hairy abdomen and legs. As your pencil gets dull, add to the softer shading of the tunnel and trap door.

   Go over outlines, darkening as necessary.

Clean up any smudges with your eraser. Put the date on your drawing and save it in your portfolio!

Knock knock.

Who's there?

Vicuña

ALWAYS SKETCH LIGHTLY AT FIRST!

Vicugna vicugna

South America: Peru, northern Chile.
Size: 1.4 m long (4.5 ft), 1 m (3 ft) high at shoulder

This smallest member of the camel family lives high in the Andes Mountains, at the edge of the desert near grasslands. Vicuñas are fast, graceful animals who live in groups of up to 15, either one male and females or all male. The females give birth to one young after a gestation period of about ten months. Though long hunted for their wool and meat, it appears that their population is increasing.

1. Sketch two *overlapping* circles for the body. Sketch two smaller circles for the head and nose. Connect head and body with long, curving lines of the neck.

2. Add eyes and nose, paying close attention to where they lie within their circles. Draw a small curved line for the mouth, and add ears.

3. Darken the eye, shade the face, darken the jaw line and make a shadow on the neck. Add jagged lines for the shaggy fur on the chest.

4. Sketch small circles for the leg joints. Draw the front legs and hoofs.

5. Add a rear leg.

6 Draw the other rear leg. Add the tail. Use short pencil strokes to outline the back. Add hair under the belly.

7. Pay attention to darker and lighter areas as you carefully shade the rest of the body. Add emphasis to outlines. Draw a cast shadow with some rocks and grass on the ground.

Vabulous Vicuña! Clean up any smudges with your eraser, put today's date on it and save it in your portfolio!

Drawing Tips

Start out loose and light

You've seen it enough times in this book: *Always sketch lightly at first.*

Sketching means trying out ideas, trying out variations, and basically not worrying too much whether the finished product is perfect.

Sketching can vastly improve your drawing skill. Try to do a number of quick sketches to get a feel for the animal: from life, from pictures, or from videos or TV. Then, using your sketch as a guide, carefully put together your final drawing.

You may find–as perhaps all illustrators and artists do–that your lightly drawn sketches have more energy, and capture more of the spirit of the animal, than your final drawing.

So save every drawing, always with the date you drew it!

Timed Drawings

Here's a challenge: pick a subject, and do timed drawings: first, ***five seconds*** (really, it's possible!). Next, do a 30-second drawing. One more: give yourself two minutes. Now take as long as you need–ten minutes, a half an hour, a day…feel the difference in each? Which is the most fun?

ALWAYS SKETCH LIGHTLY AT FIRST!

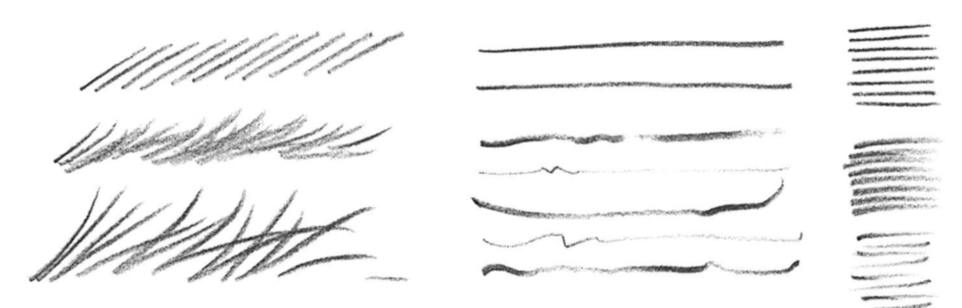

Drawing Tips

Lines make a difference

Lines are not all created equal. Some lines can make your animal come to life. Try making your lines interesting. Learn to use lines to capture the feel of the animal you're drawing. Here are some suggestions.

- **Make outlines expressive**

  How is the outline *of the animal different in each camel? Do you see a technique you can use to make your own drawing more lifelike?*

- **Create texture with lines**

  What about texture–which drawing gives you an idea what the camel might feel like if you touched it?

- **Use lines to show form**

  In addition to showing texture, how do lines help show the form (three-dimensional shape)? Can you see how lines on one of these two Bactrian camels make the drawing look more three-dimensional?

A final thought...

Save your work!

Whenever you do a drawing–or even a sketch–put your initials (or autograph!) and the date on it. Save it. You don't have to save it until it turns yellow and crumbles to dust, but do keep your drawings, at least for several months. Sometimes, hiding in your portfolio, they will mysteriously improve! I've seen it happen often with my own drawings, especially the ones I knew were no good at all, but kept anyway....

Do-it-yourself portfolio

Tape (both sides)

Cardboard

Cardboard

String (to tie portfolio closed)

Index

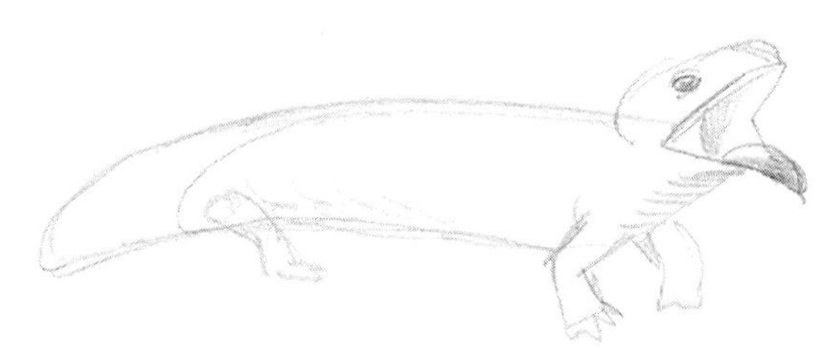

KENT
17
Learn about other books in
this series online at
www.drawbooks.com!